MASTERS OF THE MENTAL GAME SERIES BOOK

The Mental Game of Hockey

Playing the Game
One Shift at a Time

MASTERS OF THE MENTAL GAME SERIES BOOK

This book is being given to

_____

Because I care about you and your success

_____

Brian M. Cain, MS, CMAA
with Jason A. Kersner

Brian Cain Peak Performance, LLC

www.BrianCain.com

WHAT CHAMPIONS ARE SAYING ABOUT
BRIAN CAIN & *THE MENTAL GAME OF HOCKEY*

"One shift at a time. Many coaches talk about playing hockey that way. Cain gives you a simple process that any coach can follow so you can teach how to actually compete that way."

Seth Appert
Men's Ice Hockey Coach
RPI University

"Hockey is a competitive game. As coaches, we are always looking for a competitive advantage. This book gives you a competitive advantage and helps your team play their best on a more consistent basis."

Damian DiGiulian
Men's Ice Hockey Coach
St. Michaels College

"Brian Cain and *The Mental Game of Hockey* are trendsetters and game changers. This book will positively impact the way you approach the game."

Erin Wente
University of Vermont Women's Ice Hockey
All-Time Leading Scorer

"A classic that every hockey player and coach should own."

Joakim Flygh
Women's Ice Hockey Coach
Yale University

"This book is the hockey coach's Bible to developing teams with more mental toughness who compete in the moment and focus on what really matters – the next shift."

John Micheletto
Head Men's Ice Hockey Coach
The University of Massachusetts

If this book has had a positive impact on the way you coach or play hockey and if you would like to have a testimonial featured in future editions of *The Mental Game of Hockey,* please e-mail your testimonial to admin@briancain.com.

We look forward to hearing how this book has positively affected your game and life. We would also welcome the opportunity of working with you to become a master of the mental game, and to helping you DOMINATE the day, one shift at a time.

In pursuit of excellence,

Your mental conditioning coach for hockey,

Brian M. Cain, MS, CMAA

MASTERS OF THE MENTAL GAME SERIES BOOK

The Mental Game of Hockey

Playing the Game
One Shift at a Time

MASTERS OF THE MENTAL GAME SERIES BOOK

Brian M. Cain, MS, CMAA
with Jason A. Kersner

Brian Cain Peak Performance, LLC

Brian M. Cain, MS, CMAA
Mental Conditioning Coach
Peak Performance Publishing
Brian Cain Peak Performance, LLC

The Mental Game of Hockey
Playing the Game One Shift at a Time

A Masters of the Mental Game Series Book

Printed in the United States of America
Edited by: Mary Lou Schueler
Cover design & manual layout: Brian M. Cain
Illustrations: Nicole Ludwig and Greg Pajala
Photography: Paul Lamontagne

Brian M. Cain, MS, CMAA with Jason A. Kersner
The Mental Game of Hockey
Playing the Game One Shift at a Time
A Masters of the Mental Game Series Book

PREFACE

Every shift in hockey has a life and history of its own. In most games there will only be a handful of shifts that determine the outcome of that game. As a coach or player, you never know what shift will be the one that makes the big difference, so you have to treat them all as if they are going to be that big shift.

The save in the first period is just as important as the save at the buzzer against an extra attacker. All three periods equal the outcome of the game, not just the last goal scored or the final save made.

Playing the game of hockey one shift at a time is what the mental game is all about. Giving yourself the best chance for success on this shift in turn gives you the best chance for success on the scoreboard at the end of the game.

This book is an extensive collection of my experiences working as a mental conditioning coach in the game of hockey and is a body of work that, when put into action, will unlock your potential and take your game to the next level.

This is a book about the process of becoming a person, player, coach and program of excellence. It's a book about becoming a champion so that you can win more championships. This is a book designed for you to become more so that you can get more out of yourself and others. And this book will provide you with the guiding principles that will give you the best chance for success in the mental game of hockey and in the mental game of life.

The material contained herein has worked for real hockey players and coaches in real college and high school programs around the country. This is not a book on theory; *it is a book on APPLICATION! You must actually DO what we suggest in this book. Reading this book is simply not enough; YOU MUST TAKE ACTION!*

DOMINATE THE DAY!

DEDICATION

This book is dedicated to all of the hockey players and coaches out there who realize the value of the game and the amazing life lessons you learn through participation.

This book is dedicated to you, the reader, because you are committed to excellence. You have chosen to invest the time it takes to be different, abnormal and uncommon in order to take your game and life to the next level. You want more, and my mission through this book is to help you establish a process so that you can become more.

By signing your name below, you are dedicating yourself to reading and, more importantly, to applying this book and making the commitment to enjoy the journey to the summit of The Mountain of Hockey Excellence.

I _____

(print your name) have been given everything I need to become a person and player committed to excellence. I am fully capable of living the life of my dreams and leaving this world and the game of hockey more than it was when I got here. I am a one-shift warrior who lives and competes in the present and chooses to focus on the process over the outcome, and I will stay positive in the face of adversity.

Sign your name here: _____

ACKNOWLEDGMENTS

It is with sincere and deep appreciation that I, Brian M. Cain, acknowledge the support and guidance of the following people who helped make this manual possible:

Special thanks to Dr. Ken Ravizza, Dr. Rob Gilbert, Erin Wente, Kevin Sneddon, Seth Appert, John Micheletto, Damian DiGiulian, Joakim Flygh, Bruce Garrapy, and to the thousands of coaches and athletes who have shared their stories of the mental game with me and who have influenced the writing of this book.

It is with sincere and deep appreciation that I, Jason A. Kersner, acknowledge the support and guidance of the following people who helped make this manual possible:

Special thanks to Brian M. Cain; my business partner and best friend Jared Kersner; my parents Steven and Trice Kersner and sister Jana Kersner; and to my coaching mentors and good friends that have helped me grow – Luke Strand, Troy G. Ward, Cam Ellsworth, Keith Paulsen, Scott Borek, and Jason Lammers. But most importantly, thank you to the many players that I have been fortunate enough to coach; our shared experiences have helped me become a better person and driven me to learn about the mental game.

www.BrianCain.com/hockey
for BONUS Mental Conditioning Material
& FREE Peak Performance Training Tools

CONTENTS

CHAPTER #5
CHAMPIONSHIP PREPARATION 113

CHAPTER #6
PERFORMANCE ROUTINES
HOW YOU PLAY ONE SHIFT AT A TIME 131

FOREWORD

This is a book about excellence – excellence in hockey, and more importantly, excellence in life. If you have this book in your hands, it is my mission that this book will become "that book" – that book that changed your life.

I am living proof that one book can dramatically change your life.

For me, that one book was *Heads-Up Baseball: Playing The Game One Pitch At A Time* by Dr. Ken Ravizza and Tom Hanson. Reading that book changed my life as a baseball player and as a man. I was fortunate to have spent two years with Ken in his graduate school program in sport psychology at Cal State Fullerton. Those were the two most influential years of my life because of the growth, self-discovery and model that Ken set for me to follow. ***Coaches must remember that athletes need both a motto to say and a model to see***. Ken provided both of those for me.

This book contains the principles and lessons I have learned from Ken and the many other great mentors I have had in the mental game, some of whom I have met and some I have not met yet.

In most ways, this book is the product of my experiences throughout this great journey called coaching and the daily learning process. It represents the accumulation of the knowledge I have gained and wish to impart to those who strive for daily excellence and who want to become more so they can have more through the game of hockey.

Being on the bench at the Frozen Four, in the dugout during the NCAA College World Series, working with National Teams and NCAA Champions; cornering Ultimate Fighting Championship World Champions in Main Event bouts in Las Vegas; working with athletes competing for their home country in the Olympic Games; and working with coaches and athletes in Major League Baseball, the National Football League, the National Hockey League and in the National Basketball Association as a mental conditioning coach – these are just a few of the standout moments I have been fortunate to experience in my career. I hope this book helps coaches and players to get even more out of this great game and one of the greatest athletic experiences available to young people all over the world.

I am humbled by the privilege I have to live the life of my dreams, and I move forward in life with an attitude of gratitude. I understand, however, that this privilege is not guaranteed to me, and any success is the result of having had the opportunity to surround myself with successful and selfless people who have shown me the way. *I have seen further because I stand on the shoulders of giants like Ken*. It is my hope that you are able to use my shoulders to help you see further.

Human growth and development happen through experience – the experience of the events in your life, the teammates you have, the people you meet, the friends you keep, the music you listen to, and the books you read. It is my sincere hope and desire that this book becomes a life-changing experience for you on the ice and in life.

Compete One Shift At A Time!!!

AUTHOR'S NOTE

The intent of the author in writing this book in The Masters of the Mental Game Series was to create a comprehensive mental conditioning book that could be used by hockey players and coaches as their blueprint for mental conditioning and developing mental toughness. Mental conditioning and peak performance training are about searching within yourself to see what you are made of as a person and as a competitor.

When you search within yourself, you learn that all the answers to life's questions and challenges live inside you. As you work your way through this book, you will learn what drives you to embark on this self-transformative journey of self-improvement by continuously reflecting upon your attitudes and actions.

While reading this book, you will recognize the mental adjustments and changes you must make to access all the untapped and limitless potential that resides inside you. Tapping into every ounce of combined mental and physical potential is the art of peak performers, and this book will teach you this art form by coaching you to search from within.

This photo has impacted me since I first saw it in 2002, and it illustratively captures the concept of one's ability to search within oneself. My life's mission is to help you uncover the excellence that lies within you and to coach you to develop the tools necessary to achieve your best in hockey and in life by taking a look inside.

INTRODUCTION

INTRODUCTION TO PEAK PERFORMANCE, MENTAL CONDITIONING AND THE MENTAL GAME OF HOCKEY

> "Hockey is a complex dance that requires shifting from one objective to another at lightning speed. From offense to defense back to offense back to defense. To excel, you need to act with clear mind and be totally focused in the present. You must be where your skates are."
>
> **Jason Kersner**
> **Head Hockey Coach**
> **Skipjacks Hockey**

What is peak performance in hockey? What does it mean to play your best one shift at a time? What is mental conditioning and why is it essential to both understanding and answering those two questions?

This is your mental conditioning program for hockey. A 10-chapter/10-week (or 10-day if you really get after it) off-season or in-season training program that will give you the knowledge and techniques to unlock all of your performance potential on the ice.

The coaches and athletes I have worked with at national championship-winning college programs, state and national championship-winning high school programs, the Olympic Games, Ultimate Fighting Championship, National Football League, National Hockey League, National Basketball Association and Major League Baseball have all experienced one thing in common: *As you elevate to higher levels of competition, success becomes less about the physical skills and more about your mental game.*

This truth is essential to acknowledging and appreciating the importance of mental conditioning, and the more you think about it, the more obvious it becomes. At the highest levels of hockey, everyone has the physical skills to be successful or else they would not be competing at that level. Talent is just not enough. If it were, every 1st round pick in the NHL Draft would have an all-star career, but they don't. Many fizzle out and never produce at the level they or the organization had expected.

Thus, on top of developing the physical skills to compete at the highest level, coaches and athletes must devote more time to the development of their mental game that will allow them to perform consistently at their best on the rink.

To further emphasize the significance of mastering the mental game, there is a simple two-word sentence to convey the significance of mental conditioning as it relates to hockey: ***Consistency wins.***

> "Consistency is habit formed by repeated acts. Consistent behavior will get you consistent performance. Habits plus mindset make you a peak performer."
>
> *Brian Cain*
> *Peak Performance Coach*

CONSISTENCY IN TRANSITION

Consistency is the significant difference between the good and the great coaches, players and teams. Those who compete at the highest level on a consistent basis are the legendary and iconic figures in the game like Wayne Gretzky, Mario Lemieux, Nicklas Lidstrom and Jonathan Toews.

> "I have missed more than 9,000 shots in my career. I have lost almost 300 games. On 26 occasions I have been entrusted to take the game-winning shot, and I missed. I have failed over and over and over again in my life. And that is why I succeed."
>
> *Michael Jordan*
> *One of the Greatest Athletes of All Time*
> *NBA Hall of Fame*

In Michael Jordan's words of the pursuit of excellence, he said he can't accept not trying. He was an extraordinary athlete; however, he used a set of principles that laid the foundation for his successful career. He did it step by step and he was named the MVP of the NBA 5 times. However, when critics said he didn't play defense, he set his goal to be the best defensive player in the league – and he earned the 1988 NBA Defensive Player of the Year Award. He said that he couldn't see any other way of accomplishing anything except step by step. He established a process. This echoes the statement: ***Doing a little a lot and not a lot a little.***

Anyone who has the physical prowess necessary to compete has the ability to perform at the highest levels of his or her ability once in a while, but it is the one-shift warriors who stand out among everyone else – the ones who bring their best every shift and every time they step onto the ice. These are the persons who will make the biggest impact on their team, in their league, and who will ultimately have the greatest career.

WHAT MAKES THE BEST OF THE BEST

Demanding the best possible performance from your body is a characteristic of all great athletes. However, physical development to your peak potential does not come cheap.

The most competitive athletes invest significant amounts of time and energy into the many grueling hours it takes to train their bodies for performance at the highest levels of hockey. The off-season and late night workouts of Jaromir Jagr are something of legend and something that you will research on Google and use as motivation if you want to get the most out of your career. He continued to play great hockey into his forties! ***He invested his time, did not spend it.*** He had a plan and the mindset of a champion.

MENTAL CONDITIONING IS ESSENTIAL

The greatest players and teams in hockey are aware of something that you might not realize: ***If you want to be the best of the best, doing the physical training is simply not enough.***

Skipjacks hockey coach Jason Kersner has the philosophy that his team must play with great consistency; he teaches his players that they have the ability to stand straight and not sway no matter which way the wind blows. It's performing with excellence at a moment when it means the most. They know when they step over the boards and hit the ice they must be totally focused on that one shift. It's playing in the moment that shows their mental toughness. Their mental toughness training is geared toward showing players that their minds are as important to hockey success as their bodies. Thus, the best of the best know that mental conditioning is as vital to their success as physical conditioning.

THE POWER OF THE MIND

The power of the mind is as miraculous as it is incomprehensible. Studies have continued for years, and we are still miles away from truly understanding the full capabilities of the human brain. Countless examples of the "mind over matter" type of experience have been documented over time.

There are incredible examples of prisoners of war being released and performing amazing physical feats that they had practiced mentally during their detentions.

One such example is of a POW who came out of exile having visualized playing golf every day. By the time he was free and stepped onto a golf course, he lowered his golf game by ten strokes. Upon his release, another POW who practiced mental conditioning became a competent guitarist by teaching himself the guitar through repetitive visualization processes, despite never playing the instrument before.

There are endless miraculous stories similar to these, and it is safe to say that even though neurological function is not as well understood as the physiological, no one is prepared to discount the human mind as the most powerful tool available in the world.

The good news is that even without understanding the scientific intricacies of the human mind, anyone can improve his or her mental toughness for hockey with a simple mental conditioning program and by doing simple exercises on a routine basis. You learn best in conditioning yourself to be the toughest mentally just like you do physically – by *doing a little a lot, not a lot a little.*

MENTAL CONDITIONING FOR HOCKEY

Mental conditioning for hockey is the process of developing mental toughness, by which players exercise and develop the mental focus, awareness and discipline to control their mental state in order to control their behavior. *You must be in control of yourself before you can control your performance on the ice* – and gaining self-control in the fast-paced, aggressive, competitive sport of hockey is essential to your success.

When divided between the two words, mental relates to the mind, while conditioning means to train oneself to behave in a certain way or to accept certain circumstances that will happen in the game, such as an official missing a call, the other team scoring a goal, your team making several turnovers in a row or you having to play through pain and discomfort.

Mental conditioning is a process similar to how you would physically condition your body in the weight room. When you lift weights infrequently, you don't get any stronger; but when you lift weights consistently, the timely repetition will make you stronger. Mental toughness is developed the same way, *by doing a little a lot*.

Mental conditioning gives you the techniques to develop control over the beliefs in your mind. Beliefs (both positive and negative) shape our behavior, fuel our emotions, create our experiences, and determine much of our results.

THE POWER OF BELIEFS

The following is a great example of the mental game and how the process you take will affect the outcome.

Mt. Mansfield High School hockey coach Bruce Garrapy had been coaching for 30 years. His team would have great work ethics and terrific practices but time and time again they ended the season with the same results. They had years when talent carried them but Garrapy still felt like they were underachieving. He changed practice, attended clinic after clinic, purchased video after video until he had his own library of hockey videos. But the result was the same. Great practices, great kids with no better results. Something had to be causing his team to choke in the big games and play down to the levels of their competition even when they were better.

Coach Garrapy knew it had to be mental. But how do you coach the mental game? Aren't athletes just born mentally tough? If you work them hard enough, they become mentally and physically tough, right? He thought that for many years of coaching. He learned he was wrong!

The following season his team started with my P.R.I.D.E. (Personal Responsibility In Daily Excellence) program. He wrestled with the idea of giving up time on the ice or in the weight room to put time into the classroom and move from physical to mental conditioning. He had made the commitment that he was going to do this each and every day. His team was going to condition their minds just like they were conditioning their bodies.

That season the team wasn't world beaters by any means, but he could slowly see changes in the way they acted, the way they prepared for games and the way they played their games. **He knew that if they would act, behave and think differently, they would start getting different results.**

This team entered the postseason state tournament as the number 10 ranked team out of 16. In the state tournament they won their first round game and for the first time in school history won their second round game and advanced into the state semifinals. The opponent was none other than a team that had already beaten them three times that season. Coach Garrapy and the team stuck to their pre-game routines, they never spoke of the opponent at all, and their focus was on their game and their execution. **The opponent was nameless and faceless. The true opponent was themselves. To play their best hockey – that was all they could control.**

On game night they went out and played with all the confidence in the world. They played not to win the game, but to simply win a shift, one shift at a time. They did and they won a close, hard-fought game and were heading to the Vermont State Championship for the first time ever. **That night the best team didn't win; the team that won was the team that played the best.**

The key take-home point is that if they didn't believe and hadn't regained and reinforced their mental toughness, Coach Garrapy has no doubt they would not have succeeded that night.

Mental toughness training is the key to consistent success. Belief can be an incredibly powerful force. There is nothing more powerful than having a team behind you that believes in you.

The goal of this book is to give you the tools to develop your mental game, shatter limiting beliefs, develop the confidence and consistency needed to play your best one play at a time, and give yourself the best chance to win on the scoreboard and, more importantly, in life.

CAIN'S COACHING POINT:

The mental conditioning skills you will learn to perform at your best in hockey will also help you to perform at your best in life when your hockey playing days are over.

Hockey really is a gateway to life. The skills coaches teach you on the ice will help you to perform in the real world outside of hockey as well.

COACHES' BUILT-IN EXCUSE:
NOT HAVING A MENTAL CONDITIONING SYSTEM

It is an unfortunate reality that most hockey programs leave mental toughness to chance. Many coaches think that their players will either figure it out or they won't – that their players either have it together between the ears or they do not. Many coaches think players are born mentally tough or mentally weak. *This old-school thinking is actually an excuse for not knowing how to train and develop mental toughness in their hockey players.*

These coaches believe there is nothing they as coaches can do to help enhance the athlete's mental toughness other than tough physical conditioning, and yet they will agree that performing at your best when it means the most is as much about the six inches between your ears as it is the six feet below them.

This coaching mentality fails to recognize that developing a strong mental game has just as much, if not more, significant value to performance on the ice than developing a strong physical game.

EXCUSE EXTERMINATOR IN YOUR HANDS

Until now, mental toughness training for hockey has been left to chance. In this book, you will learn the importance of focusing on the **present moment** and will gain a true understanding of what it means to have a **process over outcome** approach, a **positive attitude** and **performance preparation routines**, along with the **discipline** and **dedication** necessary to achieve your hockey and personal goals, regardless of adversity and the failures you will face.

MENTAL TOUGHNESS IS A SKILL SET

Mental toughness is simply a skill set that can be taught, developed, and continuously improved just like the physical part of your game in hockey.

Mental conditioning is strength and conditioning for the six inches between your ears that control the six feet below them. **Having a mental conditioning system is essential to playing your best when it means the most, one shift at a time.** Mental conditioning will give you a skill set to be successful in hockey and, more importantly, successful in life.

To RPI hockey coach Seth Appert, toughness is the ability to focus on what is important and stay focused on the present moment.

"You can get whacked, the calls go against you, you can be physically challenged in a game – you have to focus on what's important. You cannot be deterred, intimidated or thrown off from your goal of competing one shift at a time. That's mental toughness."

Seth Appert
Head Hockey Coach
RPI University

THE 90%/10% SHIFT

Whether or not coaches and athletes understand the complete significance of mental conditioning, most coaches and athletes I have worked with will agree that training for hockey games is 90% physical and 10% mental. They acknowledge that a noticeable shift occurs when the puck finally drops. In the heat of competition they acknowledge that performance becomes 90% mental and 10% physical. This is called the 90%/10% shift to give athletes and coaches an illustrative taste of how valuable mental conditioning is when it is time to put on the uniform, lace up the skates and drop the puck.

The reality is that there should be no shift. Mental conditioning should be integrated into physical conditioning and every aspect of preparation. It should be 100% mental and physical conditioning combined, because one is never complete without the other.

This book will give you a system for training your mental game and for unlocking your true on-ice potential. As you read the book and develop your mental toughness, think about it as going to the gym to do strength and conditioning for your brain instead of your body. This book is your "Mental Conditioning Gym."

CAIN'S BLUEPRINT FOR EXCELLENCE

I always get the question, "Brian, when you work with the top hockey programs, what do you teach?"

What I teach them is the same mental conditioning program that you will learn – about exactly how to play your best when it means the most, by teaching you how to:

• Live in the present moment and compete one shift at a time.

• Act differently than how you feel and start having good "bad" days and good "bad" shifts.

• Focus on the process over the outcome.

• Identify what you can control and what you cannot.

- Have your own personal and program philosophy and core values for hockey and life.

- Challenge your limiting beliefs and your perspective.

- Stay positive in the face of adversity – and hockey is a game of adversity.

- Develop preparation and performance routines for consistent high-level hockey performance.

- Take responsibility for your performance and life.

- Relax, recover, and gain control of your thoughts, feelings and emotions before the big shift and in life.

- Recognize your signal lights and develop the awareness to win the next shift and win the day.

- Release negative thoughts and refocus back to the next shift when you get distracted and when adversity hits.

- Move from intelligence and thinking to trusting, action and positive results.

- Use mental imagery to help you prepare and be more confident for your next game and next shift.

- Inspire, lead and motivate yourself to make the impossible possible.

- Develop the dedication and self-discipline that you need to power through the grind it takes to succeed.

- Take action steps to make excellence a lifestyle, not an event.

These are the fundamentals of mental toughness and represent the blueprint I use when working with any hockey coach, player or program to develop personal responsibility in daily excellence (PRIDE).

THE GOAL OF THE BOOK IN YOUR HANDS

The goal of the book in your hands is that you learn how to control your mind so you can successfully direct your body to achieve the level of hockey and life performance necessary to become a champion.

CAIN'S COACHING POINT:

If you want to win a championship, you must first become a champion. Using the skills taught in this book will make you a champion on the ice and in life.

Always remember that if you want more wins, you must become more as an individual first so that you deserve more wins.

ONE SHIFT/DAY AT A TIME
10-WEEK PRIDE PROGRAM FOR HOCKEY

This book is written as a 10-week or 10-day program for building mental toughness for hockey, a little a lot each week.

We will focus on two critical principles of success:

1. One shift/day at a time

2. PRIDE – Personal Responsibility In Daily Excellence

The PRIDE acronym serves as the backbone of this mental conditioning system for hockey, reminding you of the significance of making excellence a daily pursuit for which you are personally responsible and accountable.

The outcome goal is that you become a peak performer on the ice and in life. Before you can become a peak performer, you must first understand that excellence is a lifestyle, not an event, and is defined as being at your best when it means the most, which is every day and every shift in hockey.

CAIN'S COACHING POINT:

Excellence is being at your best when it means the most – every shift and every day.

For a hockey player, being at your best when it means the most is every single shift. Every single rep in practice. Every single lift in the off-season. If you are a student, it's every single class. As former Green Bay Packers head football coach Vince Lombardi said:

"Winning is not a sometime thing; it is an all-the-time thing. You don't do things right once in a while... you do them right all the time."

Vince Lombardi
Green Bay Packers Football Coach
NFL Hall of Fame

Regardless of your performance arena, taking PRIDE is having an overall system for success.

CLIMBING THE MOUNTAIN OF HOCKEY EXCELLENCE

Climbing The Mountain of Hockey Excellence is a symbolic concept used throughout this book. The summit of the mountain represents your goal, a state or national championship, while the mountain represents the obstacle one must conquer to reach it, yourself and your season. The journey up The Mountain of Hockey Excellence marks the self-improvement endeavor an individual must take to become a peak performer.

CAIN'S COACHING POINT:

If you want more success on the ice, you must become more off the ice. Winning a championship is a by-product of becoming a champion.

This book employs the concept of The Mountain of Hockey Excellence to demonstrate that the achievement of performance excellence is a long, but worthwhile, journey.

Similar to mountain climbing, hockey is about training to conquer one mountain at a time. Once that mountain has been climbed, it is time to return to base camp and set your sights on the next mountain's summit and get to work. Each mountain is scaled one step at a time. It does not matter if you are climbing Mt. Everest, one of the big boys, or the local hill in your town – all mountains are claimed one step at a time and all hockey games are won one shift at a time. Base camp is your video room, practice rink and weight room. The next mountain to climb is your next game.

> "Don't measure yourself by what you have accomplished, but by what you should accomplish with your ability. Success is not how good you are compared to someone else; success is how good you are compared to how good you could be."
>
> **John Wooden**
> **Legendary UCLA Basketball Coach**

ONE STEP TO THE SUMMIT – STAY & YOU DIE

Mountain climbing also serves as a great activity to compare with hockey because when a team scales a mountain, they cannot simply live on the summit: They must return to base camp, regroup and climb another mountain, or their climbing career is over. Similarly in hockey, an individual or team cannot win a championship and be champions forever. They will forever be champions of that season, but as soon as the next season rolls around, the slate is swept clean and all the opposition is ready to become title contenders. This forces the champions to start the season anew in their quest for that season's championship, that climb's summit. Therefore, your time at the summit is only temporary.

Often in hockey seasons, a team must play on back-to-back nights. No matter what the outcome of the last game was, you must quickly let go and begin to refocus on the next game, that present moment. A hockey player clearly understands that you can't live on the summit – you must get back on the horse and ride or you will die. After the game, enjoy the win, then get back to work on the next 200 feet. The mental preparation allows you the best chance to succeed and be consistent game after game.

CAIN'S COACHING POINT:

It is key that you give yourself a certain time frame to enjoy a win or lick your wounds from a loss. Giving both a deadline where you learn from your performance and then re-engage back into the moment and into the next game gives you the best chance to prepare and perform consistently at your best.

Ultimately, there is no end to the pursuit of excellence, no one final summit to reach. ***Excellence is a constant journey that demands personal responsibility in your daily commitment***. As you read this book, the use of the mountain climbing analogy will assist your understanding and application of the mental game as you strive to become more.

WHAT IS YOUR SUMMIT?

In reading this book, it is clear that your immediate Mountain of Excellence is conquering this book to understand how to play at your best and achieve performance excellence, and how to transform yourself into a peak performer. However, it is only by fully understanding the reasons for embarking on this journey and openly recognizing the larger mountain you desire to conquer that you will make the most of your personal growth and mental conditioning experience.

Therefore, you must ***begin with the end in mind*** to give your journey a greater sense of purpose. You must know precisely where it is you want to end up and ***why*** you want to end up there, or you might find yourself climbing the wrong mountain – a mountain that your parents or someone else wanted you to climb, not the mountain you wanted to climb.

Think about your desired destination. Is it being the best hockey player on your team? Is it winning a state or national championship? Breaking a particular record? Getting the college scholarship or drafted into the NHL, or simply making the team? Whatever your journey, you must begin with the end in mind. You must have an outcome goal and a destination to start your journey.

CAIN'S COACHING POINT:

What is The Mountain of Hockey Excellence you desire to climb and conquer? What is it you want to accomplish?

_____

_____

_____

_____

_____

_____

_____

CAIN'S COACHING POINT:

Remember, you are allowed to climb more than one mountain, but should focus on one summit at a time. Keeping your mind in the present moment, sticking with the process and staying positive will help you to better enjoy your journey and experience more success than if you mountain hop and pursue different summits during the day. Whatever mountain you are climbing at that time, focus on that specific summit. Be where you need to be when you need to be there, hike one step at a time, and play hockey one shift at a time.

"The mark of a champion is pride in the preparation for competition. Champions are built, not born. There is no off-season for someone on the road to being a champion. There is only preparation and competition."

Kevin Sneddon
Head Hockey Coach
The University of Vermont

THREE STEPS TO ACCOMPLISHING ANYTHING

Most people have heard the saying **_"You can do anything if you set your mind to it"_** but are skeptical of deeming it a universal truth. Well, I am one of those people who believe that if you truly desire something, why not set your mind to it and give everything you've got to achieve it? To make your dreams become a reality you must pursue your goals in an effective and realistic manner. This is why peak performers must understand and effectively utilize the three-step process to accomplishing anything, both in hockey and in life.

The three steps that give you the best chance to accomplish anything are these:

1. Make a commitment to your goal by writing it down and putting it where you can see it on a daily basis.

2. Make it public and share your goal with your teammates, friends, family, accountability partners and the people in your inner circle.

3. Work with a relentlessly positive energy on a daily basis to make it happen – the type of relentlessly positive energy that can only be found when you are pursuing something you are passionate about and have a BIG reason why. So be very selective about your goals.

**These three steps provide you with the strategy that gives you the best opportunity to accomplish anything you desire.**

As you proceed on your journey through this book, utilize these steps to accomplish your process-based goals along the way. This is why you identified and established your mountain in the previous section to facilitate the first step of this process in your personal journey. It is your job to facilitate step number two, and it is the purpose of this book to provide the information and knowledge to facilitate step number three so that you may conquer the mountain and reach its summit.

ONE SHIFT/DAY (TODAY) AT A TIME

Now that you have established your mountain and know the three principal steps to reaching the summit, it may still appear to be an intimidating mountain to climb.   Do not be daunted by your destination.   You chose it because you want it – because a fiery passion within you burns and yearns to shed its light on the snow-capped pinnacle of your mountain.   You will conquer your Mountain of Hockey Excellence; it all comes down to taking the first step and then another and another until you reach the top.   Have patience in the process and enjoy the journey.

INTRODUCTION REVIEW

- In hockey and in life, consistency wins.

- If you want to be the best of the best, doing the physical conditioning is not enough. You must do both physical and mental conditioning.

- Peak performance occurs only when the body and the mind are working together to maximize their performance potential.

- The power of the mind is as miraculous as it is incomprehensible.

- Mental conditioning is the process of developing the mental toughness skill set by which an individual exercises and develops influence over his mental state in order to control his physical behavior.

- Mental toughness is taught, developed and continuously improved upon, just like going to the weight room for your physical toughness.

- Mental conditioning should be integrated into physical conditioning and every aspect of hockey performance. You do not separate the mental and physical conditioning; you do them together.

- PRIDE = Personal Responsibility In Daily Excellence

- Excellence is being at your best when it means the most – every single day.

- The Mountain of Hockey Excellence represents the obstacle one must conquer to reach his/her outcome goal at the summit.

- The journey up The Mountain of Hockey Excellence is a self-transformative endeavor an individual must take to become a peak performer.

- One cannot live at the summit; you have to keep hiking or you will die.

- There is no end to the pursuit of excellence.

- Peak performance is a constant journey pursuing excellence and demanding personal responsibility in this daily pursuit.

- Choose your Mountain of Hockey Excellence you desire to climb and conquer.

- Remember, you are allowed to climb more than one mountain, but should focus on one summit at a time.

CHAPTER #1

TAKING PRIDE IN HOCKEY AND CLIMBING TO THE SUMMIT OF THE MOUNTAIN OF HOCKEY EXCELLENCE

"When you fail, find the lesson in it and then recall a time when you succeeded. Then you will become both a winner and a learner."

Brian Cain
Peak Performance Coach

RISE AND GRIND

Each morning when you wake up, a new climb up The Mountain of Hockey Excellence begins. Every day it is time to rise and grind.

In your backpack are your experiences and what you have learned on previous journeys from past days. Make your journey by focusing on one day and one step at a time.

The importance of taking one day at a time cannot be overstated. One hockey coach that I work with suggests to his team that the season is a journey and it is so many miles to their postseason venue. However, they are traveling at night and their bus will only be able to see with the headlights on for 200 feet at a time. His players see that the journey has to be taken for those 200 feet, then the next 200 feet, and so on till they reach their destination, driving only 200 feet at a time.

This was a much more manageable concept for the players and coaches alike. You know your desired destination – the summit of your mountain – but you must familiarize and condition yourself with the fundamental principles necessary for survival. This must be done on a daily basis. Start by breaking the journey down into smaller chunks such as conditioning, team camps, summer workouts, regular season, and finally – postseason. *It is the start that stops most people, and the start of your day is the most important part of your day.*

As any mountain climber preparing to ascend Mount Everest can attest, one must gradually build the stamina and conditioning for the long trek to the summit. Putting in the time and establishing mental endurance is of high importance, so that you are prepared for the treacherous conditions you are bound to face on your long journey. *Embrace the adversity* and practice the mindset you need to succeed one day at a time to reach your summit.

WHAT ARE YOUR PROGRAM CORE VALUES?

As you set your sights on the summit of The Mountain of Hockey Excellence, you must begin preparing for the journey by establishing core values. *A core value is a personal belief reinforced by how you spend your time and treat other people.*

You must identify your personal and program core values in order to realize what you stand for both now and in the future. These core values will provide an internal guide to direct you on your journey and will reflect how you approach your pursuit of excellence. These values will provide your safety net for when you fall. And make no mistake – when you hike the mountains that we will, you will fall. *Falls are to be embraced, not avoided.*

CAIN'S COACHING POINT:

Reflect upon the following question: How do you want to be remembered when your last journey is over? What do you want people to say about you at the celebration of your life as a player/coach who was committed to the pursuit of excellence?

_____

_____

_____

CAIN'S COACHING POINT:

Answering the question of how you want to be remembered when your life's journey is complete will help provide clarity to what is most significant to you and how you will want to begin living your life today. It will help you clarify your core values.

As you reflect upon this big question, consider how your core values transfer to your hockey performance. Think about how you would like people to acknowledge you and your contributions to your sport and your team over the duration of the current season.

A coach I work with has his team visualize the season and then write a newspaper article summary of the season as they would like for it to transpire. At another classroom session, prior to the first game, he will have them write a brief speech for the end-of-season banquet and let them present it to their teammates for their vision of how the team and players will be honored at that banquet. This mental imagery provides the players insight on the goals for the season but doesn't lose sight of achieving them step by step, 200 feet at a time.

He also has his team members write down their daily goals in their *Brian Cain Peak Performance Notebooks* at the start of practice and show them to their position coach. Periodically during practice, the coaches refer to these goals for the day for their set of players to reaffirm focus on their individual goals. The players must be instructed on how to set daily goals and how to be specific in their goals to sharpen their mission at practice.

Simply writing down "Get Better" doesn't define a player's goal for improvement because the players will write down what they think the coach wants to hear. They must be very specific in their mission for that day's practice and training session.

DIFFERENT VALUES FOR DIFFERENT TIMES

The reason we transition focus to a set of core values for the present (off-season into the season or vice versa) and not for an entire lifetime or calendar year is that a lifetime or calendar year is a daunting time frame. A lifetime or year is too difficult to imagine and therefore presents an intimidating mountain to climb. *It is important to focus on how you want to live over the course of the season in order to focus on how you must live in the present moment.* Establishing this perspective will make climbing your mountain appear much more manageable.

Once you have identified what you want people to say about you and you have reflected this in your core values, start living by them "Today." These core values are fundamental principles that should be integrated into the routines of your daily life. If you are not regularly practicing these values, you will end up losing your way to the summit. If you are only focused on the summit of the mountain, then while you are climbing the summit you will surely miss a step and fall. Thus, be in the present moment in your climb and you will reach the summit.

CAIN'S COACHING POINT:

The secrets of success are hidden in the routines of our daily lives. You will be as successful as your routines allow you to be on a daily basis. Start establishing routines and habits of excellence.

APPLYING CORE VALUES TO LIFE

When you look to the future, you may think it is difficult to have integrity for your entire life or to be responsible for your entire life or to have self-discipline for your entire life. This may be true, but you CAN live with integrity, responsibility and self-discipline "Today."

With this perspective, you have an appropriately sized mountain to climb "Today." And then, do it all over again when tomorrow becomes "Today." The end result is **today + today + today = your career/life.**

To begin applying core values to your sport and life, choose one or two and focus on them for a set period of time.

CAIN'S COACHING POINT:

I recommend working on your specific core values for 4-5 weeks. It takes 21-28 days for positive personal change to occur with a focused plan and accountability partner. Right now, look over your core values and ask yourself, "How do I apply my core values in my life at this present time?"

Imagine it is the month of December and one of your core values for December is being self-disciplined. As you commit yourself to working on your self-discipline this month, think about the following:

How would I define self-discipline?

_____

_____

What does self-discipline look like in the different aspects of my life?

If I am an athlete or a coach, what does self-discipline look like in competition, in training, in academics, at the nutritional table, in recovery, and in my personal life?

COMPETITION: _____

TRAINING: _____

ACADEMICS: _____

NUTRITION TABLE: _____

RECOVERY: _____

PERSONAL LIFE: _____

To provide myself a point of reference and to give me a chance at living that way, how do I identify specifically what it is to be self-disciplined in those areas?

Answering all of these questions is significant to defining exactly what it is and how it is you plan on living this core value. If you specifically outline your core values, you give yourself the best opportunity to live them.

By establishing what it looks like for you to live your core values, you set yourself up for success. **It is easier to act your way into thinking and feeling than it is to think and feel your way into action.**

Knowing what action you must take and how you will take it to become the new-and-improved version of yourself sets the stage for a successful journey up the mountain.

When establishing your core values, I suggest you focus on between one and three for a given period of time. Initially, setting more than three would be an overwhelming endeavor. Giving yourself a more narrowed focus will increase your chances for successful mastery of a particular core value. If you can focus on self-discipline for the month of December, you are going to have the skill of self-discipline beyond December into January. You may work up to having five or six core values over time. As with most anything, start small, get some summits/wins under your belt, and then go bigger.

SUCCESS LEAVES CLUES

Here is some insight into achieving a successful career in anything you do: **Success leaves clues.** If you want to be a millionaire, go hang out with people who are millionaires. If you hang out with people who are making $50,000 a year and you tell them you want to make a million dollars a year, what are they going to do? They are going to laugh at you, because they do not see it as a reality. If you go hang around people who make a million dollars a year, you will get some ideas on how to make your first million.

The same rationale is true for hockey. You always hear coaches telling players, **"If you want to get better, play with people who are better than you."** This is because when you play with better players, you begin to pick up the clues to their success. Imitation and adaptation to higher levels of competition will ultimately lead to your own performance improvement and success.

"We cannot become who we need to be by remaining what we are. We must either grow or we will die. We must grow or we will get passed by."

Brian Cain
Peak Performance Coach

SURROUND YOURSELF WITH BETTER STUDENTS

To further illustrate the importance of hanging out with the right crowd, I will share a personal story from high school. When I was a high school student, I was not great academically. I reached a point where I knew I needed to improve my grades to play college sports. I made a self-improving adjustment in my life and began surrounding myself with those who were academically more successful. I started to study with my teammates, mainly Tony Coudert, one of the greatest teammates of all time, who helped me to become a better student. Rather than go play video games, I would go to his house or the library, and soon I became a much better student.

CAIN'S COACHING POINT:

If you want more in a certain area of your life, you must become more. You become more by associating with those who are more than you in that area. You will become the average of the five people you associate with most. Choose wisely.

I didn't feel like going to the library, but I went anyway. The students that went there after school had a pre-established discipline that I knew I needed to develop.

I began noticing their study habits, and I started to learn that there are techniques you can use that are very simple to help with memorization and knowledge acquisition. When I began to imitate them, I started to get better results.

Success is largely about discovering a winning formula and implementing the system that facilitates excellence. Mastering the mental game is no different. If you surround yourself with those devoted to performance excellence, your chances of achieving it will drastically improve. When you invest your time properly into a winning system in the pursuit of excellence, success will take care of itself.

> "If you're bored with life – you don't get up every morning with a burning desire to do things – you don't have enough goals."
>
> *Lou Holtz*
> **ESPN analyst and former college football coach**

DAILY GOAL SETTING & TIME PRIORITIZATION

Beyond the establishment of core values, daily goal setting and time prioritization are important for establishing the routine discipline necessary for peak performance. *I used to call it time management, but have since learned that you will manage your time based on how you prioritize your time*; therefore, *time prioritization is one step before time management. A great way to prioritize time is a daily planner broken down in fifteen-minute segments and planned out the night before so that you maximize every second of your day.*

CAIN'S COACHING POINT:

There is only ONE factor among all the hockey players in the world who are competing for what you want. You all have only 86,400 seconds in a day. Most will spend time; you will INVEST time. If you are not efficient with your time, the competitors who are will pass you by. Learn to take control and advantage of your time, or your time will take control and advantage of you.

A lot of hockey players spend very little time on their fundamentals – instead, they work on breakaways or flashy moves when sound fundamentals would be a great investment of their time. Thus, they find themselves somewhere close to the middle of the ladder of success, usually falling short of their potential. If they are halfway on the ladder, then they are as close to the top as they are to the bottom. If you spend your time unwisely, you are moving down the ladder of success. However, if you invest your time, then you can move up the ladder of success. Either way you are getting better or becoming worse – you can't stay at the same place on the ladder. *INVEST YOUR TIME; don't spend it.* And make sure you know what your outcome goal is, what you are after, so that when you reach the top of your ladder you are sure it is leaning on the right wall.

As an aspiring peak performer, you must find different ways to make the best investment of your time to accomplish the daily goals you set. Throughout this book, I will share with you techniques you can use to better invest your time. An example of a great technique for time prioritization is to take a dry erase marker and write on your bathroom mirror what you want to accomplish the next day.

I started doing this when I was in college and have found it to be a VERY effective technique. **When you look in your mirror, you are not seeing who you are. You are seeing who you are working to become.**

You are in your bathroom frequently throughout the day and the writing on your mirror will remind you constantly of what you want to accomplish. It also provides an effective method of preparing for the next day. When you go to bed, you will be relaxed knowing you already have a jump-start on the next day. By simply preparing the night before, your daily goals will always be waiting for you on your mirror when you wake up.

CAIN'S COACHING POINT:

Champions prepare their day the night before. Be sure that you pack your bag; then lay out your clothes, breakfast and everything you need to start the next day with TOTAL DOMINATION before you go to bed.

THREE STEPS TO PERFORMANCE IMPROVEMENT

Whether it is practicing core values or prioritizing your time, peak performance is all about continuous personal development and necessary change. *A key theme throughout this book is that if you want more, you must become more.*

Championship-winning coaches and athletes know that they must first become champions of personal responsibility in daily excellence before winning championships. They also know this takes an understanding of how to make necessary adjustments to change their performance to attain successful results.

One of the most successful mental conditioning coaches was the late Harvey Dorfman, author of *The Mental Game of Baseball* and mental conditioning coach to some of the greatest athletes in the world. Having spent some time with Harvey, he taught me that there are three essential steps you must follow if you want to make a performance improvement:

1. Develop an *awareness* of what needs to change.

2. Develop a *strategy* for change.

3. *Implement the strategy* with an accountability partner.

Most athletes fall short of significant performance improvement because they either lack the awareness of what they need to change, do not formulate an effective strategy for the change, fail to facilitate the strategy to bring about the necessary change, or have a "YES" partner rather than an accountability partner who tells them the truth. Without this three-step system of performance change, an athlete can never achieve the necessary performance improvement to achieve excellence.

PERFORMANCE CHANGE: WINNERS & LEARNERS

In our culture today, much importance is put on winning. If I asked you to fill in the blank in the following phrase, what would you say? There are winners and _____. Most people would say *losers*, but what needs to be in that blank is *learners*.

It should read *winners and learners*. How does this relate to the 3 steps of performance change? We need to develop a winner's mindset – this is where the mental game is as important as physical training.

So **step one** is that you must unlearn what you have learned. Identify what needs to be changed and make the person aware of that change. Next, whether you are a coach, player, employee or parent, there are four words that can bring out the best in someone.

"I believe in you."

Four simple words that a person needing to change must hear. It can mean all the difference in the world going from the fear of failure to the **DO**.

In a classic line from the movie *Star Wars,* when Luke fears failure, Yoda tells him, **"Do or do not – there is no try."** By saying *I believe in you*, you are telling your players that you have their back, that you are going to push them and be there for them, that they are not walking this road alone, and you will allow them to do things that they thought were impossible to do.

The **second step** is deciding on the strategy that will make this person successful. If you can't coach or motivate a player to do what needs to be done, then you must coach or motivate that person to follow through on what he or she can do. A coach once told me that his greatest satisfaction as a coach was seeing a player become a vital part of the team and growing into a person that may not be the best athlete on the team on any given day but always plays his or her best when the team needs it the most. The biggest hurdle for you as a coach, player or parent is finding the right strategy to push those buttons of change for that individual in a positive manner.

The **third step** is implementing the strategy. When you improve a little each day, eventually big things occur. We refer to this change over time as *The Compound Effect.* Just think for a moment – if you get .5% better each and every day, in just two months you are 30% better. So for example, when you are conditioning a little each day, eventually you have a big improvement in conditioning. Not tomorrow, not the next day, but eventually a big gain is made.

Don't look for an instant change in performance physically, but seek the small improvement one day at a time. That's the only way it happens – and when it happens that way, it lasts.

Individuals making a performance change should have an accountability partner that they are accountable to who tells them the truth. First, there has to be a mental change, a mindset shift; they must believe in what needs to change. Secondly, they must buy into the strategy of how to change. And lastly, they must actively participate in implementing the strategy.

After completing these three steps, you will find that you have both a "**winner and a learner.**"

SELF-ASSESSMENT: STOP – START – CONTINUE

In order to further initiate your personal development and facilitate the accomplishment of your goals, you must assess yourself to build self-awareness. As an aspiring peak performer, you must assess your most recent performances to establish self-awareness of what you must improve in your pursuit of excellence. Take a look at your last three days. What are some actions or behaviors that you need to STOP in order to achieve the goals that you have set?

CAIN'S COACHING POINT:

What I must STOP doing in order to achieve my goals:

1)_____

2)_____

Now, I want you to write down what it is you must START doing to help you achieve your goals.

CAIN'S COACHING POINT:

What I must START doing in order to achieve my goals:

1)_____

2)_____

Now, I want you to write down what it is you must CONTINUE doing to help you achieve your goals.

CAIN'S COACHING POINT:

What I must CONTINUE doing in order to achieve my goals:

1)_____

2)_____

The Stop, Start, and Continue activity is a very simple process that ought to be frequently practiced to provide self-assessment and to keep you moving up your mountain. It is a simple activity to keep yourself honest about your work effort, but it is often not performed enough.

SIMPLE vs. EASY

It is here that I will take a moment to address an important distinction in both mental conditioning and performance in general. For any performer, it is important to be aware of a very significant distinction between the words "simple" and "easy." **Simple and easy are not synonymous**.

Just because something is simple in concept does not mean it is going to be easy to do. If all simple things were easy, everyone would perform their best each time out and no upsets would ever occur. There would be no reason to play the game on the ice – you could play it on paper.

There are a lot of average people walking around who have excellence buried inside of them but are not trained or are not willing to harness their hidden, untapped potential. As you read this book, you must consistently work to adopt and implement the simple practices and techniques that make a significant difference in performance.

THE NEXT 200 FEET

Imagine you were to hike from base camp to the top of The Mountain of Hockey Excellence – the tallest mountain in the world. If you were to leave base camp at midnight, could you hike to the top of The Mountain of Hockey Excellence on the trail that takes you to the summit? The answer is a definitive "Yes." It will be dark out, but you have the ability to hike the entire way up the mountain in complete darkness because of your headlamp. Your headlamp allows you to travel anywhere in the dark, because it illuminates the next 200 feet of the path. Therefore, by simply focusing on the next 200 feet, it is possible to hike through the darkness to the summit.

When you are hiking the next 200 feet, animals may attack you. You may take a wrong turn, you may challenge Sasquatch with some beef jerky, and/or you may roll an ankle. These events symbolize the adversity you are sure to face on your journey, and they are all outside of your control. All you can do is **embrace the adversity** and do what is necessary to reach your destination.

DESTINATION DISEASE

When metaphorically hiking up the mountain, the biggest obstacle we face is our obsession with the end result, the destination. This destination disease is representative of whatever end result you desire – the championship, the first line, a particular stat line, the perfect season or the Hall of Fame. Remember that *the destination is the disease and the journey is the reward.*

Excessive focus and time devoted to looking at the destination beyond the next 200 feet is a common illness. People set their goals too far out in front of them without understanding, creating and implementing a process to get there. By focusing on the outcome, people become stationary dreamers as opposed to advancing toward their goal, 200 feet at a time.

This is, quite simply, inaction versus action: the dichotomy between thinkers and doers. This is the condition of people counting down the days until that dream comes true as opposed to making the days count in a proactive and productive pursuit of that goal or dream. A dream without action will remain a dream, while a dream that motivates action has the opportunity to become a reality.

As you proceed through each chapter of this book, remember to focus on the next 200 feet as opposed to the summit of your mountain. This will prevent you from being overwhelmed at times and will make the ascent appear more manageable. *Keep the process over the outcome and the journey over the destination.*

REFUSE THE URGE TO BE AVERAGE

As you start to apply the strategies in *The Mental Game of Hockey* to your life, you will receive some criticism, and some people may make fun of you for your commitment to self-improvement and performance excellence because it is different and abnormal to be committed to excellence. *If you want different results, you must act and think differently.* Do not listen to the voices of negativity, for they are the voices of the masses – they are the voices of the average.

Average people and average teams are the best of the worst and the worst of the best. Do not settle for average; strive for excellence and set your sights on the summit. Reach the pinnacle of success by climbing The Mountain of Hockey Excellence with a focused determination on your goals and with a dedication to personal responsibility in your daily excellence. *Hike that next 200 feet and you will learn there are no traffic jams on the extra mile.*

START YOUR JOURNEY WITH ONE STEP

The rest of this book is devoted to the 10-week journey of excellence within the PRIDE program. The material within these chapters will give you the mental conditioning skills to establish your blueprint for excellence. View each chapter as if it is the next 200 feet and conquer the mountain that is this training program. It is a journey that will begin during fall preseason and hopefully culminate with a state or national championship. Regardless of when you start the journey, however, this program will provide you with the knowledge and skills to make the progress necessary to reach the summit of your mountain.

IF IT IS TO BE, IT IS UP TO ME

Remember, YOUR OWNERSHIP of this program is what will make the difference. You can't just read the book. You must OWN THE BOOK. You must put this book into action.

The most powerful two-letter-word sentence in the English language summarizes what this journey is all about: *If it is to be, it is up to me.* Your success in hockey and in life is determined by a lot of factors, and no factor is more important than the person reading this right now... YOU!

It has been said that *it is the start that stops most people.* Do not wait. Get started. RIGHT NOW!

Remember, if you take the four middle letters out of "DoN'T WAit!" you get "*DO IT!*"

So don't wait, *DO IT!* Get started on your journey up The Mountain of Hockey Excellence, TODAY!

CHAPTER #1 REVIEW

- PRIDE = Personal Responsibility In Daily Excellence

- Excellence is being at your best when it means the most – every single day.

- The Mountain of Hockey Excellence represents the obstacle one must conquer to reach his/her outcome goal at the summit.

- The journey up The Mountain of Hockey Excellence is a self-transformative endeavor an individual must take to become a peak performer.

- One cannot live at the summit – you have to keep hiking or you will die.

- There is no end to the pursuit of excellence.

- Peak performance is a constant journey pursuing excellence, and demanding personal responsibility is this daily pursuit.

- Choose your Mountain of Hockey Excellence you desire to climb and conquer.

- Remember, you are allowed to climb more than one mountain, but should focus on one summit at a time.

- The Three Steps to Accomplishing Anything:
  1. Make a commitment to a goal.
  2. Make it public with an accountability partner.
  3. Work with a relentlessly positive energy today.

- Today is where we are, every day.

- A core value is a personal belief and virtue reinforced through a commitment to yourself and your team.

- Live your core values.

- It is easier to act your way into thinking and feeling than it is to think and feel your way into action.

- Success leaves clues.

- Surround yourself with those who are better than you.

- Take advantage of your time or time is going to take advantage of you.

- The Three Steps of Performance Change:
    1. Awareness
    2. Strategy
    3. Implementation of the strategy

- Frequent self-assessment is essential to establish performance awareness.

- Simple and easy are not synonymous.

- Focus on the next 200 feet of the task at hand.

- A dream without action will remain a dream, while a dream that motivates action has the opportunity to become a reality.

- Do not settle for average – it is the best of the worst and worst of the best.

- It is the start that stops most people, so get started TODAY!

CHAPTER #2

PRESENT-MOMENT FOCUS
ONE SHIFT AT A TIME

> "OBSTACLES are those frightful things you see when you take your eyes off your goals."
>
> **Henry Ford**

THE NEXT SHIFT

Hockey is a fast-paced, continuous game in which there are no built-in breaks like there are in football and baseball. In hockey, the transition time for players is faster than any other sport; the average length of possession is 4.7 seconds per team. Players transition from offense to defense and defense to offense at any moment, and have to do so many times on each shift. The game of hockey is so fast-paced, and transition happens so rapidly, that you must stay focused on the present moment and not the past moment. What's important NOW (#WIN) is the next play and next shift in the game.

In the introduction, you learned about the mindset of peak performers. You started to identify your values and put your focus on the plan as to how you will climb your mountain. You learned the importance of concentrating on the next 200 feet and the process it takes to climb to the summit. As a committed athlete and someone who wants to develop mental toughness, you must understand that *you do not count the days – you make the days count.*

How do we actually make the days count? The first step is possession of a present-moment focus.

THE 30-SECOND DRILL

Before discussing the present, I want you to experience it. In the following exercise, I want you to live in the present moment by immersing yourself in a present-moment focus. This exercise was taught to me by my mentor, Dr. Ken Ravizza, and it is called the 30-second drill.

Now as you read this, I want you to invest 30 seconds of your time as if your life depended on what you were reading. Sit up straight in your chair with your feet flat on the floor and LOCK IN! Now, I want you to look at each word and hear it as if I am there inside your head speaking to you.

I want you to read every word with a commitment that if you could regurgitate what you just read, you would win a million dollars. Think of it as the Million Dollar Mentality, because when you engage and focus with this type of intent all the time, it will not be long before someone wants to pay you a million dollars to work with them.

Ready?

Give me 30 seconds.

GO!

For a short period of time you can do anything you want with your levels of attention, energy, and focus. Right now, the focus you are reading with is different than it was 10 seconds ago – feel that.

You see, you are more locked in right now than you were 15 seconds ago – recognize that. You are currently demonstrating your ability to be into the present moment and play one shift at a time.

If you can focus like this without someone having to ask you, that is the result of a present-moment mental toughness. So, while you read this chapter today, I want you to come back to this level of focus as many times as you can and lock in for 30 seconds at a time.

That is 30 seconds.

You are allowed to space out for a moment.

Whew... I hope you felt the intensity of those 30 seconds.

If I asked you for 10 minutes of total undivided attention with that level of focus, you'd probably say: "Cain, that is crazy. There is no way I can read with that intensity for 10 minutes." I would agree.

Break 10 minutes into 20 30-second segments and now it's more manageable. And I think you would agree that 30 seconds is a good shift length in hockey. So you can train yourself to be totally locked in for the duration of your shift.

Challenge yourself to become a student of the mental game, someone who is totally immersed in the present; and when you get distracted or space out, recognize that you are distracted. Then release and refocus back into the present.

When you think of the present-moment focus, if something positive or negative happens in the game, you have to move on to the next play without lingering over the last play. If you turned the puck over or missed a good scoring chance, you don't have time to react to that last play by throwing up your hands or having bench eyes – you must then refocus on the next play. If you don't move on to the next play, you will most likely commit more mistakes or errors that will lead to further erosion of your potential success in the game.

Essentially, it is a much shorter version of the 30-second drill that players use as a part of their routine to get into the present moment.

As you read this chapter, you will develop an enhanced understanding as well as the mental skills of present-moment focus. It is important to remember that you can get here, the present moment, anytime you want. It is all a matter of awareness and choice.

> "You are trying to get players to understand that how they play is a lot more important than whether or not they win."
>
> **Jason Kersner**
> **Head Hockey Coach**
> **Skipjacks Hockey**

HOCUS-POCUS or FOCUS-REFOCUS

Realize that success in any endeavor is not the product of hocus-pocus. You are not going to be successful today because the moon and the sun and the stars and the galaxy just happen to line up for you. *You are going to be successful to the degree that you are able to focus and then refocus when you become distracted.*

Success is not hocus-pocus magic; it is actually much simpler than that. Success is largely dictated by your ability to maintain present-moment focus on the tasks at hand. The key to developing an intense and productive focus is to recognize when you become distracted, take a deep breath, and then refocus your attention.

You will get distracted, because everyone does. The attainment of peak performance is contingent on the development of distraction awareness. *You must develop the ability to recognize when you are distracted and then refocus back into the moment.* An easy way to remember this is to think, *If I want to win, I must focus on **What's Important Now** (#WIN).* Focus on what you are doing right here in this moment and on accomplishing the tasks in the present moment. This is the focus of performance excellence and successful progress.

WATCH OUT FOR FISH HOOKS

Through recognizing that we all get distracted from time to time, it is equally important to recognize what distracts us from our goal. The term "fish hooks" is symbolic of the negative thoughts from external stimuli that your mind can get caught on during your pursuit of excellence.

Fish hooks represent distractions beyond your control that you focus on, which deplete your energy and rip you away from performing your best and living in the present. Examples of fish hooks could be obnoxious fans, poor officiating, unprofessional coaches, irritating teammates, past mistakes, etc. – all of which are outside of your control.

Ultimately, fish hooks are a hassle and a needless waste of your time. You must develop an awareness of them so you do not get hooked, and so that when you do, you can get off the gaff (what they call the barb on the fish hook in the angler's world) before getting ripped out of the water.

To further illustrate the application of fish hooks in performance, think of yourself as a fish. As a fish, you are swimming in a school up Black Puck River to the destination of Lake Excellence.

As you swim upstream, you need sustenance for your journey, so you dine on whatever you can find. You discover worms are an especially delicious but a rare treat. You have observed some of your friends trying to eat worms dangling in the water, only to get stuck in the mouth with a fish hook.

You learn you must be wary of fish hooks when you see a worm. If you accurately identify fish hooks with worms, you can actually still have a meal by eating around the hook. ***Thus, if you keep the presence of mind to inspect your worms carefully, you will give yourself the best chance to reach Lake Excellence, aka play your best in the midst of the chaos called the game of hockey.***

In this analogy, the worms are the opportunities to learn and succeed on your journey to performance excellence, and the fish hooks are the external stimuli within those opportunities that could keep you from your forward progress. As a performer (or fish), you must stay in the present moment and strategically seize the opportunities for self-improvement.

Hall of Fame Coach John Wooden said: "Failure to change is often just stubbornness that comes from an unwillingness to learn, an inability to realize that you're not perfect. There cannot be progress without change, even though not all change is progress. Failure is not fatal, but failure to change might be."

So control what you can control and change what you can change. Focus on what you can control – your presence of mind – and work around the fish hooks that have the potential to hold you back. If you see the worm but forget to check for a fish hook, then you are bound to get hooked.

Be aware of fish hooks. ***Do not get hooked.***

CAIN'S COACHING POINT:

I want you to identify three fish hooks that you deal with on your team. What distractions have a tendency to steal your focus and get you hooked away from the present?

FISH HOOK #1 _____

FISH HOOK #2 _____

FISH HOOK #3 _____

USING CONCENTRATION GRIDS

Concentration grids have been a staple of mental conditioning for years. This game/exercise is all about concentration and efficiency, which are best accomplished by staying in the present moment and going one number or one shift at a time. Concentration grids are a great way to increase your ability to stay in the present moment for an extended period of time, as you will need to be able to do to play your best hockey.

ONE NUMBER. ONE SHIFT AT A TIME.

Your training program with concentration grids is simple. Cross out the grid numbers from 00-99, in order, as fast as you can. During this exercise, you are testing yourself to see how efficiently you can perform the task. You are also testing your ability to concentrate and stay in the present.

Start practicing this exercise in a quiet environment to become comfortable with the activity and to monitor your present-moment focus. Once you have become proficient at it in a quiet environment, you may play music or do this activity in front of the TV as a way to include distractions, just as there will be when you compete. The more you do this activity and the more quickly you can cross out the numbers in order, the more you are developing your ability to concentrate and keep your mind in the present moment.

Get to the rink a few minutes early – a great time to do a concentration grid is in the rink when another team is playing or practicing, with all of the action and noise, before you go into the locker room and change from your street clothes into your one-shift warrior uniform.

Hockey players I have worked with report that the grids allow them to become more aware of when they start to space out and lose focus in school and on the ice. They become more aware of when they slip out of the present and into the past or the future. This exercise also allows them to become more aware of when they are trying too hard and need to take a breath in order to relax and get back into an optimal level of focus.

MEASUREMENT = MOTIVATION

It is also important to keep track of the time it takes to complete each grid. When I started doing concentration grids on a routine basis (Monday, Tuesday, Thursday and Friday mornings before I ate breakfast), my time was in the low- to mid-teens in minutes. After almost two weeks, I was able to do them in about four or five minutes, even in the crazy and chaotic environment known as a high school cafeteria.

Here is a sample concentration grid you can use to help train yourself to stay in the present moment for an extended period of time.

CAIN'S COACHING POINT:

Yesterday is a cancelled check, tomorrow is a promissory note, and today is cash: Invest it wisely.

Yesterday is history. Tomorrow is a mystery. Today is a gift; that is why we call it the present.

Brian Cain Peak Performance, LLC
Concentration Training Grid
www.BrianCain.com

86	54	04	72	20	05	34	79	52	17
73	43	50	70	44	12	28	59	94	35
45	62	63	97	51	95	91	67	84	75
27	69	23	00	08	83	09	41	65	78
80	39	68	47	29	93	36	30	38	42
61	53	19	48	49	74	40	18	15	21
60	01	14	22	64	07	58	02	32	16
13	31	26	71	66	33	06	85	10	89
76	46	98	37	99	24	57	11	55	82
92	25	81	96	87	88	77	03	56	90

Brian Cain Peak Performance, LLC
Concentration Training Grid
www.BrianCain.com

86	54	04	72	20	05	34	79	52	17
73	43	50	70	44	12	28	59	94	35
45	62	63	97	51	95	91	67	84	75
27	69	23	00	08	83	09	41	65	78
80	39	68	47	29	93	36	30	38	42
61	53	19	48	49	74	40	18	15	21
60	01	14	22	64	07	58	02	32	16
13	31	26	71	66	33	06	85	10	89
76	46	98	37	99	24	57	11	55	82
92	25	81	96	87	88	77	03	56	90

CHAPTER #2 REVIEW

- [ ] Yesterday is history, tomorrow is a mystery, and today is a gift – that is why we call it the present.

- [ ] Do not count the days; make the days count.

- [ ] The present moment is a matter of awareness and choice.

- [ ] Success in athletics is not hocus-pocus. It is all about your ability to focus and refocus.

- [ ] Focus on WIN (What's Important Now).

- [ ] Beware of fish hooks and things you cannot control.

- [ ] Train your present-moment focus by using concentration grids.

- [ ] The time is now and the place is here.

CHAPTER #3

PROCESS OVER OUTCOME

"The biggest battle on the ice is the one between style and efficiency. A particular shot or way of moving the puck can juice the player and stir the crowd, but the efficiency of performance is what wins the game for the team. Style must never overwhelm the fundamental goal of playing the game and winning."

Jason Kersner
Head Hockey Coach
Skipjacks Hockey

The ability to perform at a level of excellence on a consistent basis is the goal of all peak performers. As the previous chapter discussed, the maintenance of a present-moment focus will assist you in this goal; however, you must have something to focus on in the present moment during performance. **This something is the process.**

A peak performer's focus must always be on the process. By keeping focus on the present elements of the performance process, athletes give themselves the best opportunity to perform on the level of excellence. An excellent process will yield excellent results, and performing a step-by-step process directed at excellence will get you up the mountain. Remember, the commitment and concentration on the next 200 feet of the hike will get you safely to your destination. Focus on being excellent on your journey step by step up The Mountain of Hockey Excellence and you will be sure to reach the summit.

UNLEARN WHAT YOU HAVE LEARNED

The current hockey society we live in is a results-driven society. If you are a coach reading this, you will not likely have a job if you do not win games. The kicker is that to win games you must not focus on winning, but on the process of winning. Coaches and athletes I work with most often unlearn what they have learned to focus on in their sport – mainly winning and focusing on other outcomes that are outside of their control vs. processes that are within their control and that give them the best chance for success.

A peak performer must understand that winning is the outcome of performance excellence – thus, the product of an individual's or team's performance. The focus of the individual athlete and team, therefore, ought to be their performance, because that is what is truly within their control and yields the desired outcome. More precisely, a performer's focus should be on the process of his performance and directly on what he can control to provide the best opportunity for success.

CAIN'S COACHING POINT:

You must often unlearn what you have learned and realize that what got you here might not get you there. You must always be asking yourself, *is this the best way?*

THE LAW OF AVERAGES

Former Louisiana State University head baseball coach Skip Bertman was a true Master of The Mental Game and won five national championships in 1991, 1993, 1996, 1997 and 2000. Bertman also hired Nick Saban and Les Miles as LSU's head football coaches when he was the athletic director at the school. Bertman is a man defined by excellence, and he stressed the importance of the process, emphasizing that anytime you compete there are only four possible occurrences:

1. You can play well and win.
2. You can play well and lose.
3. You can play lousy and win.
4. You can play lousy and lose.

Bertman called these the law of averages because if you play your best, you give yourself the best chance to win – BUT you are not guaranteed to win even if you do play your best. **What he knew was that he never had control over the outcome of the game. All he had control over was how prepared his team was come game day and then how they played.** Through this understanding, Coach Bertman knew that the process of performing excellently was what won games, not a focus on winning games. As a coach, he made the law of averages swing in his favor by emphasizing the process of performance excellence and execution on each pitch/each play over the outcome of winning. You can swing the law of averages in your favor as well, if you commit yourself to the process.

THE BEST TEAM NEVER WINS

I have had the wonderful privilege of getting to know and work with Ultimate Fighting Championship Welterweight Champion, Georges St. Pierre. Georges is one of the best athletes on the planet, and a large part of his consistent success has been his ability to stay focused on the process of becoming the best fighter he can be (the journey) while letting go of his desired outcome to be and maintain the status of world champion (the destination).

By focusing on the process of being the best he can be through constantly evolving as he aims for self-improvement and personal progress, Georges gives himself the best chance to retain his World Championship title every fight. Georges realizes that even though he is one of the best fighters, if not the best fighter, on the planet, he can get knocked off the summit of the mixed martial arts mountain known as The Ultimate Fighting Championship on any given night inside the Octagon. He has learned the hard way that ***the best fighter never wins – it is always the guy who fights the best***.

"I truly believe that I am the best fighter in the world. And in every sport it is the same story. It is not the best team that wins in basketball; it is the team that plays the best. It is not the fastest horse who will win the race; it is the horse who races the best. And Saturday night, even though I believe that I am the best fighter in the world, the guy who's going to win the fight is the guy that will fight the best. I am very glad to fight Josh Koscheck. He's the number one contender right now, so I want to get back to what I lost and I will go step by step in the process. I am very happy to fight him."

Georges St. Pierre
Ultimate Fighting Championship
Welterweight Champion
2008, 2009, 2010 Canadian Athlete of the Year
UFC 74 Pre-Fight Press Conference

This quote is from Georges on the eve of his UFC 74 fight with Josh Koscheck, his first fight after losing his World Championship to Matt Serra at UFC 69 on April 7, 2007. I love what he says about how the best fighter never wins, that it is always the one who fights the best. I hope you can see that he clearly understands the value of the process.

CAIN'S COACHING POINT:

St. Pierre saying "I go step by step" illustrates the mentality and focus on the process as well. When he says, "I am the best fighter in the world," he displays his confidence in his abilities – but he also recognizes that "the guy who's going to win the fight is the guy that will fight the best." This truly emphasizes his mental ability to separate the outcome from what he must do to achieve it. A total focus on the process.

The same logic can be applied to any form of competition. You may be the defending state champion or part of the best program in your area, but during competition inside the boards, it does not matter who is more talented or who has a more impressive resume. *In the heat of competition, all that matters is who competes at the higher level, who executes and plays better.*

If you are the underdog and your whole mentality revolves around you playing your game regardless of the accolades and accomplishments of your opponent, then you have done what I call "released your mental emergency brake," enabling you to play your game at the highest level, one shift at a time.

"DO or DO NOT – there is NO Try."

Yoda
Star Wars – Episode V

WHY UPSETS HAPPEN

To further challenge and change your perspective on the old cliché that "the best team always wins," let's reflect upon some of the great moments in sports history.

If you are reading this book, surely you are familiar with The *"Miracle on Ice"* in the 1980 Winter Olympics between the Soviet hockey team and the US hockey team: The Soviet team consisted of seasoned professional athletes while the US team consisted of amateur collegiate athletes.

The whole world expected the Soviet team to come out victorious. The Soviets had destroyed the same USA team in an exhibition game 10-3 in Madison Square Garden on February 9, 1980, just days before the Olympics started. We all know, however, that the end result was anything but what was expected. The US team's 4-3 victory over the Soviets will go down in history, undisputedly, as one of the greatest upsets of all time. Clearly, the Soviets had the better team, but it was the US team that won. Why? **They played better!**

Another prime example that defies the "best team always wins" cliché is Super Bowl XLII between the New England Patriots and the New York Giants. The Patriots had accomplished an undefeated season (16-0) and reached the Super Bowl with a cumulative record of 18-0. This Patriots team was hailed by analysts as arguably the greatest NFL team ever and was the 12-1 favorite to be victorious in the big game. The victory, however, went to the undaunted Giants, who led 17-14 as time expired. Who was the better team? The Patriots. Who played better on that night? The Giants.

Yet another example of a phenomenal upset is the 1985 NCAA Men's Division I Basketball Championship between the Georgetown Hoyas and the Villanova Wildcats. The Georgetown Hoyas were the defending national champions and the No. 1 ranked team in the nation, led by Patrick Ewing, the 1984 tournament's Most Outstanding Player and one of the most dominant players in college basketball history. The Wildcats were unranked in the regular season with a 19-10 record and received an at-large bid as a No. 8 seed in the tournament.

In the National Championship game, Villanova went on to play an excellent game against a team most thought to be unbeatable. The Wildcats shot an historic 79 percent from the floor as they defeated the Hoyas 66-64 to become the lowest seed in NCAA basketball history to win the national championship. Who was the better team?

Georgetown. Who played a better game that night? Villanova. There are plenty of examples from the NCAA Basketball tournaments; recently, in 2014, Mercer upset #3 seed Duke 78-71.

In boxing, James "Buster" Douglas, the unknown 42-1 underdog, defeats Mike Tyson. In Olympic wrestling, unknown US wrestler Rulon Gardner defeats Russian wrestler Alexander Karelin, who was previously undefeated in 13 years of international competition. Appalachian State beats The University of Michigan in one of college football's great upsets. The list goes on and on.

All of these upsets are sufficient evidence to conclude that the old cliché "the best team always wins" is false. The main reason is that the more talented teams often get so caught up in the outcome that they forget about the process to achieve what they desire. They shortchange their preparation, and as Super Bowl XLVIII Champion and Seattle Seahawks quarterback Russell Wilson always says, *"The separation is in preparation."*

> "Even when you've played the game of your life, it's the feeling of teamwork that you'll remember. You'll forget the plays, the shots and the scores, but you'll never forget your teammates."
>
> **Terry Lovelette**
> **Goalie Coach**
> **University of Vermont**

CONTROL WHAT YOU CAN CONTROL

The peak performance athletes that best understand the significance of the process over the outcome have established proficiency for recognizing what they can control and what they cannot. It is amazing how many hockey players still get hung up and hooked on things outside of their control. If you want to be a peak performer, you must learn how to differentiate between what you can control and what you cannot control.

A huge part of the process is controlling what you can control (your performance) and letting the outcome take care of itself – and when the "best teams" show a mental lapse, the underdog is usually right there ready to seize the moment. We can, thus, definitively state that the best team/athlete never wins; it is always the team/athlete that plays the best.

When you put time and energy into things you cannot control, you are wasting both of those valuable resources. Focusing on these things is self-defeating and assists the opposition in the process. Peak performers do not play that way; they stay locked in on what they can control.

Here is a list of things you cannot control in hockey: You cannot control the officials, the fans, the media, the other team, playing time, the ice conditions, the schedule, statistics, coaches, parents, and most of all, the outcome of the game. The only thing you can control is yourself and your APE. APE is an acronym for your attitude and appearance (body language); your positive self-talk, presence (focus), process (preparation), performance (how hard you compete), perspective; and your effort, energy and emotions.

HOCKEY AND THE CONTROLLABLES

One of my favorite sports I use to illustrate just how little control an individual has while participating in competition is hockey. Hockey is a crazy game. You can virtually do everything right and still lose. There are also days where you can do very little right and win.

Sometimes, you and your teammates can execute the game plan to perfection and meet the performance goals that the coaches have set for the team during the game, but a bad call or an unfortunate bounce of the puck can completely undermine the team's effort. On the other hand, you can fail to meet your coaches' goals but get a break here or there that keeps you in the game. **Hockey is an unfair game. So is life. Get used to it, and stop saying "that's not fair."** According to English Premier League champion head coach Sir Alex Ferguson: *"Life isn't fair. It becomes fair only when you realize it is unfair. Once you know it isn't, you're on a more level playing field, and you're better prepared for it."* Whining about how unfair things are may get you sympathy from your parents, but not when you are trying to reach the summit and win on the ice. *So get the "H-helplessness/have-to mentality" out of whiner and become a winner.*

CAIN'S COACHING POINT:

Are you that bad of a hockey coach or a player that you have to feel good and have every call go your way to win? If the answer is no, say *SO WHAT, NEXT SHIFT* the next time a call does not go your way.

You can make excuses or you can make it happen; you cannot do both!

In hockey, as in life, when you focus on the process of playing the game one shift at a time and let the outcome take care of itself, you will give yourself the best chance for on-ice and scoreboard success. Winning is a by-product of executing the fundamentals and focusing on the process over the outcome. You cannot control winning. If we could control winning, somebody would go undefeated every year because they would figure out what it took to do so and then proceed to do it. In the game of hockey, there are just too many variables that you cannot control. Focus on the process and put yourself in a position for excellence, and the process will eventually reward you with success.

CAIN'S COACHING POINT:

As mentioned above, a huge component of the process is controlling what you can control. In the space provided below, write down in the first column all of the things that you can control when playing hockey, and then list the things that you cannot control in the second column.

CAN CONTROL   **CANNOT CONTROL**

_____   _____

_____   _____

_____   _____

_____   _____

_____   _____

CAN CONTROL

CANNOT CONTROL

_____ _____

_____ _____

_____ _____

_____ _____

_____ _____

_____ _____

_____ _____

_____ _____

_____ _____

Look at the list of things you cannot control. If you choose to focus on these things, you will inevitably beat yourself. If you choose to focus on these things, you are getting hooked. You must keep your focus on what you can control.

APE

As a peak performer, you must focus your attention on what is within your control. External adversity is a part of life – you make the choice of how you react to it. APE provides you with a reminder of just what it is you have the ability to control.

APE is an acronym to remember that you control:

A – Your attitude and your appearance (body language)

P – Your perspective (how you see things),
the process (how you choose to play), your preparation,
your presence (focus) and your self-talk (positive)

E – Your effort, your energy, and your emotions

This acronym is symbolic of the concept "control what you can control." This concept is a fundamental skill of mental conditioning. Self-control is essential to peak performance, and by the end of this program you will fully understand why it is that you only have control over yourself in the midst of performance. As my mentor Dr. Ken Ravizza would say, **you have got to be in control of yourself before you can control your performance** and **you have very little control of what goes on around you but total control of how you choose to respond to it** and **your goal must be in your control.**

MY GOAL MUST BE IN MY CONTROL

All athletes and coaches will agree that goal setting is a critical part of the process in climbing your mountain of excellence. When setting performance goals, you must remember that **your goal must be within your control. A common mistake made in goal setting is setting performance goals that focus on the desired outcome instead of setting goals that reflect the process that you must execute to get that desired outcome.**

THE ONE-SHIFT PROCESS FOR A FORWARD

In hockey, a forward should not set a performance goal of how many points he or she should score (outcome), but should instead set a performance goal of shots attempted from the "scoring area," grade A scoring chances, 2nd chance pucks, etc. (process). Understand the distinction between focusing on just getting points and doing things that will allow scoring to come. For instance, if you are a "playmaker," your goal shouldn't be to get assists. Even if you make a perfect pass to a teammate backdoor, the player receiving the pass may not score – so you don't have control of the assist. Proper execution results in the player being rewarded for making good plays instead of just being rewarded for points scored. Your goal should be to make the correct read, understand the game time situation, and execute the play in a fundamentally sound manner to result in the desired outcome.

Remember, your performance goal must be within your control. If you are a "playmaker," focus on making a play, not just on getting assists. You could make a great read and a perfect pass but still have it result in a turnover because your teammate didn't make the play on his end. You should see this as a success because you executed your job – you just did not get your desired result.

You can also make a lousy play and still end up with a point, and you should see this as falling short of success because you did not execute your process. Even though you got the desired result, your performance was less than excellent; you did not execute the play correctly but were bailed out by poor defensive execution or a superlative play by a teammate. You just got lucky. By setting your performance goals on making quality plays, you acknowledge and focus on what you can control and what gives you the best opportunity for performance excellence.

By understanding exactly how your game is played – all the real causes and effects of performance within your sport – you can direct your focus to the process of your performance. This knowledge cuts out all the unnecessary elements of the game that most people harp on and gives you a direct route to peak performance. This is what it means to have an understanding of the process when you set performance goals. This is a terrific example of *"**PROCESS OVER OUTCOME.**"*

CREATING AND USING YOUR PERFORMANCE ABC's

One of the most effective strategies to help you focus on what you can control, and to create an effective process to help you play in the present, is an exercise called Performance ABC's.

Performance ABC's are three keys that can be mental, physical, or a combination of the two that you repeat to yourself, visualize, and think about before and during competition. These ABC's of your performance will keep you focused on the process you need to follow to be successful.

There are many aspects of performance that athletes may think about at times during performance, from physical mechanics to game strategy, to the opponent, to issues in personal life or other distractions happening off the ice. Setting ABC's will help keep your mind focused on the proper process for your performance based on the key elements on which you want to focus. This strategy will give you the best chance for success.

Here are some samples of Performance ABC's that I helped create with a top Midget AAA program. You can see that we set general Performance ABC's for the program, offense, defense, special situations and coaches.

Setting Performance ABC's for the program and units helps give the team a common focus on the process during competition. It also benefits each athlete and coach to set individual ABC's as a way for them to better identify the individual processes they must follow to give themselves the best chance for success.

I challenge you to create your own Performance ABC's for your position. Choose categories that apply to your position and determine an effective set of ABC's that will reflect the performance demands of those categories.

NAME	A	B	C
PROGRAM	Belief in self, teammates, system	Be the toughest, most disciplined, most selfless team	200 feet at a time
OFFENSE	Aggressive = pucks and bodies to BLUE	Hard over pucks, we want possession	Play in "5's" to generate grade A chances
DEFENSE	Create turnovers through our energy	Deny middle of ice – first 3/ last 3 strides	Play HARD – win 1st battles
SPECIAL SITUATIONS	Detail in Line changes – short and hard	Power Play = SHOOT with net presence	Penalty Kill = 3+1 pressure into 200 ft. clears
COACH	Be the fountain, not the drain	Focus on your position group during the game; control what you can control	Let 'em play; remind them to BREATHE

THE BEST COACHES FOCUS ON THE PROCESS

The best coaches and athletes in hockey know the value of focusing on the process. They see the process as a staircase they climb each day. They know what their desired outcome is and focus on that outcome 20% of the time, while focusing 80% of the time on TODAY and the steps they must take to get the outcome they desire.

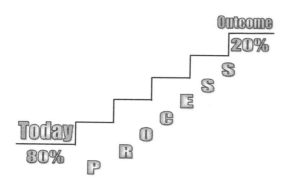

THERE ARE NO LITTLE THINGS

It is worth emphasizing explicitly that there are no little things in the pursuit of excellence in hockey. Excellence in small things is excellence in all things. As alluded to in the previous section, one must also recognize and appreciate all the little details of peak performance within hockey in order to become a peak performer. When you are fully committed to the process of becoming a peak performer, you must be aware of all the details of your performance process, for they are necessary to make a successful journey to the summit of The Mountain of Hockey Excellence.

SABAN IS A MASTER OF THE MENTAL GAME

One of the most successful coaches in college football is Nick Saban, who won the BCS National Championship at LSU in 2003 and at Alabama in 2009, 2011 and 2012. Take a look at a quote from his book *How Good Do You Want to Be?*

"Becoming a champion is not an easy process... It is done by focusing on what it takes to get there and not on getting there."

"It is done by focusing on what it takes to get there and not on getting there" – **that is committing yourself to the process.**

My challenge for you is to begin committing yourself to the process. Start evaluating your performance on the process it takes to perform at a level of excellence. Focus on the effort you give every day and, most importantly, every shift. Focus on executing the fundamentals when you perform in practice and during competition. As a hockey team, focus on playing with great energy and intensity, supporting teammates from the bench, and always demonstrating strong body language. All the physical mechanics of your sport and all the elements required for the performance of your sport matter, and performing them all excellently is what makes a peak performance.

CAIN'S COACHING POINT:

What are some aspects of the process that, if you focused on them, would give you the best chance to perform at your best?

1) _____

2) _____

3)_____

KEEP YOUR LOWS HIGH AND YOUR HIGHS LOW

Emotional consistency is essential for on-ice success in hockey. The goal of those striving for success in any arena is to maintain performance excellence day in and day out. The control of emotions is imperative for consistent peak performance.

When you are faced with adversity and your performance is not reflective of your potential, it is crucial to take a step back from your performance and focus on the process of excellence. ***Command your emotions by reminding yourself to control what you can control; and focus on releasing the mental bricks that can weigh on your mind by having a physical release that you can use, such as removing your gloves in between shifts, wiping the snow off your stick blade, taking a sip of water and spitting it out, and taking a deep breath.***

Resist the pressure to personalize performance and remember hockey is what you play, not who you are. By paying attention to the process and not the outcome, you give yourself the best opportunity to achieve excellence, because if you focus on the process and make the necessary changes to it, the result will take care of itself.

The same systematic process is true when you are performing at your best. When you are performing at your highest level and achieving success through performance excellence, it is crucial that you not become complacent. Resist the urge to buy into the hype. Do not think that a little success suddenly renders you more valuable than the process that got you there. Cemeteries are full of irreplaceable men and women. Stay humble. Continue to work the process. Give yourself the best opportunity to maintain the excellence you have been achieving by identifying the process you followed to get there, and then keep refining that process by making it more efficient and excellent.

Take a look at a "sign of success" from the one of the top hockey programs in the country. This image is testament to the program's understanding that you must focus on the process of becoming a champion in order to win championships.

It is challenging to commit oneself to the process of performance excellence. The journey is long and hard, full of obstacles and detours, but this is what makes the glory of achieving performance excellence all the more glorious. *Remember, nothing worth having comes easy. Your enjoyment in the end will be a direct reflection of the effort you had to give in the process of becoming who you needed to become to be worthy of getting what you wanted.*

> "There are plenty of teams in every sport that have great players and never win titles. Most of the time, those players aren't willing to sacrifice for the greater good of the team. The funny thing is, in the end, their unwillingness to sacrifice only makes individual goals more difficult to achieve. One thing I believe to the fullest is that if you think and achieve as a team, the individual accolades will take care of themselves. Talent wins games, but teamwork and intelligence win championships."
>
> *Jason Kersner*
> *Head Hockey Coach*
> *Skipjacks Hockey*

DEVOTE YOURSELF TO THE PROCESS

Commitment to the process of excellent performance will give you the best opportunity to achieve your goals. In this chapter, you have learned that when you devote yourself to the process, you focus on the aspects of performance within your control as opposed to the elements beyond it. You now understand that maintaining control of the process of your pursuit of performance excellence is a means to getting your desired outcome and end result.

Unfortunately, it is common for most people in hockey to be become fixated on the goal/outcome/end result of performance. As an aspiring peak performer, focus on what you need to do to achieve the outcome and results you desire. Devoting yourself to the process of performance excellence will undoubtedly give you the best chance to win and, more importantly, reach the summit of The Mountain of Hockey Excellence this season and in your life.

CHAPTER #3 REVIEW

☐ Unlearn what you have learned about winning.

☐ Process should always be placed before the outcome.

☐ Performance Excellence is greater than Winning.

☐ Know the four possible performance outcomes and the Law of Averages.

☐ The best team never wins. It is always the team that plays the best.

☐ Control what you can control.

☐ Develop self-control over your APE.

☐ Winning is a by-product of excellent execution of the fundamentals and focusing on the process over the outcome.

☐ Establish your Performance ABC's.

☐ There are no little things.

☐ Keep your lows high and your highs low – emotional consistency is essential for peak performance.

☐ Make "signs of success."

☐ Nothing worth having comes easy.

☐ When you devote yourself to an excellent process, the result will take care of itself.

CHAPTER #4

POSITIVE MENTALITY

"The Master Mind principle: Two or more people actively engaged in pursuit of a definite purpose with a positive mental attitude constitute an unbeatable force."

Napoleon Hill
American Author

The power of positive self-talk with a positive mentality makes a huge difference in an individual's performance. It is a simple concept that is both useful and effective. Having a positive mentality is so simple that it is often overlooked. We're used to hearing people tell us to "think positive" prior to performance or in the heat of competition, but the words often roll in one ear and out the other without our full appreciation of the true value in this all-too-simple piece of advice.

Having positive self-talk *(the voice inside your head, the voice you hear as you read this)* with a positive mentality is a mental skill that requires proper mental conditioning to utilize its power. The magnificent quality of positivity is that everyone is capable of it. It is simply a mental attitude that is conducive to growth and excellence through the expectation and perception of favorable and beneficial results. This chapter is devoted to conveying the importance of positivity in performance while presenting you with the strategies you need to develop your own positive mentality.

THE PROPHECY OF THOUGHT

The basic tenet is that whatever the mind expects, it will attract. This "law of attraction" has been proven with neuroscience. Thoughts manifest through actions and affect outcomes. If you are doubtful you will accomplish a task, you drastically increase the likelihood that your actions and effort will reflect that doubt, thus ensuring the failure of accomplishment. Similarly, if you possess a positive mentality when faced with a difficult task, you dramatically increase the likelihood that your actions and effort will reflect that positive attitude, and you will succeed.

The successful accomplishment of a task, however, is not guaranteed by positive thoughts. All a positive mentality does is significantly increase the probability that you will walk away from the task, successfully accomplished or not, with greater experience and with greater peace of mind. In this way, a positive mentality makes a significant difference between educational self-improvement (growth) and self-stagnation (death). Thus, your mentality represents the ultimate self-fulfilling prophecy. Thoughts become things (#TBT).

THE STORY OF ROGER BANNISTER

On May 6, 1954, Roger Bannister, a British medical student and avid runner, did the previously unimaginable. From the start of archiving world records and modern time-keeping in track events, no one had been able to break the seemingly impassable barrier of the 4-minute mile. His story demonstrates the prophecy of thought and the power of positive belief.

At the age of 25, the British sports media had already discovered Bannister, who had become one of the most scrutinized track athletes in the United Kingdom. His speed in the mile and 1500-meter events drew initial attention to his talent, but when he declined the 1948 Olympics in London to concentrate on his training and medical studies, he drew the criticism of British track enthusiasts. In 1951 Bannister won the British title in the mile, but his fourth-place finish in the 1500-meter race at the 1952 Olympics in Helsinki – the result of a last-minute schedule change that compromised Bannister's preparation routines – fueled further scrutiny for his unconventional training regimen.

After the media publicized his Olympic performance as a failure, Bannister resolved to redeem himself by breaking the seemingly unbreakable 4-minute mile barrier. He increased the intensity of this training, but not the duration, and saw steady improvements in his times, all while he continued to be a full-time medical student. In fact, the duration of his training was less than an hour per day, because he wanted to focus on his study of neurology. Bannister, however, was committed to his new goal and *loyal to the process* he felt would get him there. He was convinced that as long as he continued to see gradual improvements in his times, he would maintain his own training regimen.

The opportunity Bannister had been training for arrived on May 6, 1954, in a meet between the British Amateur Athletic Association and Oxford University at the Iffley Road Track in Oxford, England. Running mates Chris Chataway and Chris Brasher exchanged setting the pace for Bannister's first three laps. Bannister unleashed his kick in the last lap, finishing it in less than a minute before he broke the tape and collapsed in the arms of the gathered crowd at the finish line.

The announcer affirmed what the crowd of roughly 3000 spectators already knew.   To thunderous applause it was announced that Bannister ran 3:59.4 – the unbreakable record had been broken and Roger Bannister had made history! He had made the impossible possible.

DEFEATING LIMITING BELIEFS

The 4-minute mile story, however, is not simply about the historic moment of a broken world record. *The story of Roger Bannister is about breaking mental barriers and defeating limiting beliefs*. At the time, the world of track and field believed the 4-minute mile was an insurmountable human barrier, an impassable obstacle that could not be breached. The critics said it couldn't be done and that it was physically impossible to run a mile under four minutes. It was thought that the heart would stop, the brain would explode, and the lungs would collapse.

As the world scoffed at what it saw as an amateur athlete's unachievable dream, Bannister hardened his resolve to the pursuit of excellence. What makes his feat even more remarkable was that he was dedicated to attain excellence not only on the track, but also in his academic ambitions of becoming a doctor. Bannister believed in himself and he believed in the process to which he had committed himself. As long as steady small improvements accrued, he knew the outcome he desired would take care of itself – and that is exactly what happened.

After the myth of the 4-minute mile had been debunked by Bannister, other runners around the world began breaking the 4-minute mile barrier. The week after his historic performance, Bannister and two other runners ran a sub-four-minute mile. Over the course of the following year, thirteen more runners broke the barrier. Within the next two years, exactly 134 runners ran a mile under 4 minutes, and today over 20,000 have been recorded. On July 7, 1999, Hicham El Guerrouj of Berkane, Morocco, ran the current world record in 3:43:13. In 1997 Daniel Roman of Kenya ran two miles for the first time ever in under 8 minutes, in a time of 7:58:61.

This is evidence that there are no physical barriers, only self-limiting barriers. We are the ones who put up these barriers within our own psyche because we choose the beliefs of those around us. You need to unlearn these limitations and realize that once mental barriers are lifted, anything is possible. Peak performers and champions perceive the world differently, and as perspectives change, the realm of possibility expands. My goal for you is to have no mental barriers, to believe you are capable of anything you desire and work toward using the right strategies.

Bannister proved all the naysayers wrong with his positive mentality and self-belief, and now is the time for you to do the same.

> "Winners can tell you where they are going, what they plan to do along the way and who will be sharing the adventure with them."
>
> **Denis Waitley**
> **Motivational Speaker**

SELF-IMAGE OF EXCELLENCE

The field of peak performance has substantiated the notion that, as a performer, you will never outperform your self-image. If you believe you are slow, you will perform slowly. If you believe you are fast, you will perform at a fast pace. Therefore, positive thought processes, combined with clear goals and right strategies for how to accomplish them, will give you the best opportunity for success. In this way, staying positive is symbolic of belief in yourself.

A self-image of excellence is absolutely necessary if you are to embark on the quest to conquer The Mountain of Hockey Excellence. You must believe in yourself and your ability to improve throughout the process you have established to achieve your goals. You must believe in your inner excellence and its transcendence to the performances you give on a day-to-day basis. Self-image is a powerful tool in peak performance, which is why it is so important for you keep it positive.

INTRODUCTION TO SELF-TALK

When you are playing your best, what are you thinking?

_____

_____

When you are at your best, what types of words are going through your head? What's that self-talk like?

_____

_____

In peak performance, the little voice talking inside of your head, sometimes becoming outwardly expressed thoughts directed at yourself, is referred to as self-talk. During performance, this little voice inside your head talks to you constantly. You may be reading this and thinking: "What is this 'voice' Cain is talking about? I do not talk to myself, only crazy people do that." That would be the voice to which I am referring.

CAIN'S COACHING POINT:

When referring to self-talk, I often use the analogy of your two mental assassins. You have a green assassin that helps your performance and a red assassin that crushes your performance. You must train your green assassin to win the battle between your ears with positive self-talk.

Everybody has/does self-talk. As an expression of thought, self-talk embodies your mentality towards your performance. We use self-talk to motivate ourselves and to calm ourselves down when stressed. We use self-talk to encourage ourselves to become fascinated and, unfortunately, it can be used to discourage ourselves when we are frustrated. Self-talk is a reflection of self-image.

When you are performing on the ice or in the classroom, the voice in your head is either working for you or against you. Some people visualize the contrasting tones of voice as two little people on your shoulders battling for control over your conscience. Recognize, however, that this self-talk is yours. You own it; you are in control of it.

Six-time college football national champion Bear Bryant understood better than anyone the importance of positive self-talk. He was once asked how some of his most seemingly undermanned teams kept coming away with victories over bigger, faster and stronger opponents. The Bear's answer was simple and straightforward: *"Life's battles don't always go to the stronger or faster man. But sooner or later, the man who wins is the man who thinks he can."*

HARNESS YOUR SELF-TALK

Mastering control of your self-talk can be a challenge. Imagine your self-talk is a mustang (the horse, not the car), wild and spirited, seemingly uncontrollable. Now, imagine yourself as a cowboy who does not wish to strip this wild animal of its fiery spirit, but you do want it to work for you to enhance your pursuit of excellence on the open plains – so you must gain control of the animal without taking away its aggressiveness. This is how to think of your self-talk. It is an untamed and powerful beast that has the potential to significantly improve your performance.

Many of the hockey players I work with describe their self-talk as a high level of aggressiveness but always under control. They often describe it as living and competing on the edge. One player said, **"If I am not competing on the edge of my emotions and energy, highly engaged but on the controlled side of the line, I am taking up too much space."**

As a hockey player, your self-talk can be thought of as a:
 – Relaxed aggression
 – Relaxed intensity
 – Controlled rage
 – Controlled emotions

To effectively harness your self-talk, you must follow the three steps of performance improvement as earlier discussed. The first step in the process of channeling the power of your self-talk is to establish an awareness of its power over the mind. During performance, try to recognize when you use it and what mentality it reflects – positive or negative. Notice particular situations that bring it out, both the good and the bad. Notice the particular tones and language used. This is all in an attempt to understand your mental state during time on and also away from the rink.

Once you have developed a proficient awareness, the next step in effectively harnessing your self-talk is through a technique called confidence conditioning.

FOCUS ON WHAT YOU WANT VS. WANT TO AVOID
THE PINK ELEPHANT

Has anyone ever performed the mind tease on you where they instruct you to focus on something and then say, "Whatever you do for the next 10 seconds, do not think about a pink elephant"? Well, naturally the image of a pink elephant pops into your head and you have difficulty focusing on whatever it was you were told to focus on.

This little mental tease exemplifies the importance of an individual's ability to keep a focus on what you "want vs. want to avoid" because **the brain does not recognize the negative connotation of "do not" and only sees the image of that pink elephant.**

The key to ignoring the pink elephant is developing the ability to focus on what you are trying to accomplish, not what you are trying to avoid. If you are a hockey player, think about executing your position instead of trying to do someone else's role. If you are a goalie, think about watching the puck all the way into your glove and saying "catch" as you catch the puck instead of trying to not drop it. Academically, when you are taking a test, you want to focus on solving the problem or answering the question at hand, one question at a time, not worrying about the next question till you finish this one. These general scenarios represent the present-moment focus that makes the difference between subpar performance and performance excellence.

By channeling your self-talk and focusing on what you want vs. what you want to avoid, you will be competing with a positive mentality that will keep you locked into the present moment, giving yourself the best chance for success. The ability to focus on what you want with positive self-talk instead of what you want to avoid is a discipline developed over time. This process is dependent on the establishment of routines, such as practicing your self-talk and strengthening your self-talk through the use of confidence conditioning statements.

CONFIDENCE CONDITIONING STATEMENTS

Confidence conditioning statements are a mental conditioning technique used to harness the power of self-talk to work in your best interest. Confidence conditioning is accomplished by simply writing down a list of statements that give you a sense of strength and empowerment when you read them. You can put these confidence conditioning statements on notebook covers, on the wall, on your mirror with a dry erase marker, in your locker, on little cards to carry in your wallet, on your wristband, or set them as the background on your iPhone. You can put them anywhere and everywhere.

Even though you may not be aware of it, you have been using confidence conditioning statements ever since you could talk. Every time you expressed your belief in the truth of an idea or an experience, you were conditioning it. Mental imagery, which is simply the creation of vivid mental images, is a natural process as well. Whenever you imagined something or looked forward to it, you were using imagery and conditioning your subconscious mind. Confidence conditioning and mental imagery are used by a wide variety of people from virtually every walk of life and in every profession. They use these techniques because they are simple to learn, even easier to perform, and they work!

When written and/or put on audio, confidence conditioning statements are your custom-made blueprint for personal growth and mindset achievement, providing a consistent state for your mental imagery and personal development. They are goal statements that help you imagine and realize positive change with minimal stress. If you use them correctly and consistently, they will help you create the athletic career, relationships and life you most desire.

In order to be effective, confidence conditioning statements must be written and used in a way that has the desired impact on your subconscious mind. They must be brief, usually a short sentence, and phrased in the first person present tense. They must be positive, specific and realistic. You want to include as many details as possible when writing and they should carry an emotional charge. If they do not make you feel anything, they probably will not help change anything either. *The test of whether a confidence conditioning statement is written the right way is to ask yourself, "Can I read, picture and feel this statement?"*

CONFIDENCE CONDITIONING GUIDELINES

The following are guidelines to help you better write your confidence conditioning statements:

First Person: Confidence conditioning statements are tools that help you to change your self-image; therefore, it makes sense to mentally condition for yourself, because your statements are always about you. They will usually begin with "I."

Present Tense: Use the present tense (I am, I have, etc.) because, in your subconscious, the future and past do not exist. Subconscious time is always "right now."

Positive: Condition and image what you want, not what you do not want or are trying to change. Do not phrase a statement in the negative, such as, "I no longer get anxious when I go on the ice for the last shift of a big game." Instead say, "I remain calm, in control and focused on what I want to do on this shift, when the game is on the line." This focuses on what you want to do in the present with a positive mentality.

Indicate Achievement, not ability or potential: In other words, do not say "I can." You already have the potential to change your performance. Instead, create words that describe the end result you want as if it has already happened by using "I am."

No Comparisons: You are unique and have your own process of personal development, growth and change. Do not compare yourself to anyone else or measure your abilities against anyone else's. Just aim for and condition performance change in your own self-image and self-belief.

Vivid & Descriptive Language: In order to "convince" your subconscious that your confidence conditioning statements are real, your language and the images they invoke must be as vivid as possible. Be sure to choose words that help you to really "see" what you are describing.

Emotional Language: Use words that spark an emotional response to make your statements more believable to your subconscious. The more emotion you generate, the faster the change you seek will take place. Describe how you feel about your achievement.

Realistic/Accurate: Do not affirm change that isn't possible or realistic for you. Set your sights neither too high nor too low. Stretch your comfort zone a bit, but do not aim for anything you cannot honestly see yourself achieving. Remember, peak performance is a process. Do not aim for perfection; aim for excellence.

Balance: Make sure that the various goals you condition are in balance with each other. Do not overemphasize any one area while ignoring others in which growth would be beneficial. Strive for balanced growth and a balanced life.

Confidential: Without intending harm, others may remind you of your old self-image, or they may feel threatened by your desire to change. Keep your statements confidential. You may confide in coaches/mentors, if they understand the confidence conditioning process and are supportive of the changes you are trying to make for the sake of your performance.

TIPS FOR WRITING EFFECTIVE CONFIDENCE CONDITIONING STATEMENTS

1. Change Your Beliefs Before Your Behavior:

It is pointless to condition new behavior when the underlying beliefs driving your old behavior remain unchanged. Write your confidence conditioning statements for both internal beliefs and external behaviors. Failure to change underlying beliefs is one of the main reasons why confidence conditioning will not work for everyone.

BEHAVIOR: I spend an hour of quality one-on-one time with one of my teammates every weekend to strengthen our bond together.

BELIEF: More pressure on an already jammed-up schedule. I'd rather be hanging out with my friends who are not on the team than with my teammates all the time. When do I get my quality time away from my sport?

Do you see the problem? If the underlying belief does not change, it will be impossible to sustain the new behavior. As long as it feels like something you "have to" do, and not something you "want to" do, your creative subconscious will find ways to get you out of it. Try this as an alternative:

BEHAVIOR: I enjoy spending an hour of quality one-on-one time with one of my teammates every weekend.

BELIEF: I look forward to spending time with my teammates every weekend because it is fun, leaves me feeling great about our team, and is building strong relationships that will help us to perform better on the ice.

2. Build Personal Value in Your Confidence Conditioning Statements:

The positive emotions you feel as you repeat and picture your statements is what makes them "take" in your subconscious. For example:

BELIEF: My health and fitness are major priorities in my life.

BEHAVIOR: I am creative at finding ways to exercise at least one hour a day, six days a week, and I generally eat only nutritious, low-fat foods.

PERSONAL VALUE: Because I exercise and eat right, I feel energized, strong, in control, and excellent.

3. Review Your Statements to Imprint Confidence into Your Subconscious:

Imprinting is simple: READ or LISTEN to your confidence conditioning statements, PICTURE them in your mind, and FEEL the personal value (positive emotions) connected to them. The best times to do this are just after awakening and just before sleep. Review your statements twice a day at a minimum, although more often is better. Make sure you are relaxed (take several deep breaths) and free yourself from distractions. Limit yourself to 5-10 statements to start – you can add more later. Remember, it is the start that stops most people, so take the initiative and get started NOW!

CONFIDENCE CONDITIONING WORKSHEET

What do you want to change?

_____

Describe the way it is right now:

_____

Why is it a problem?

_____

How do you feel about the way it is?

_____

Describe your own behavior(s) that you want to change:

_____

What are your deepest beliefs about this situation? Be honest with yourself:

_____

Describe the way it will be after the change(s) you seek (use present tense):

_____

Describe the way you will behave to generate the result you want (use present tense):

_____

What beliefs will you need in order to support these new behaviors (use present tense)?

_____

How will you feel when you bring your vision into reality? What is the personal value for you?

_____

PERFORMANCE CONFIDENCE CONDITIONING STATEMENTS

Use the confidence conditioning worksheet to help you create your confidence conditioning statements. Look at what you wrote on the worksheet. If your answers accurately express your own goals and feelings, use these examples as models for creating your own powerful confidence conditioning statements.

Remember, you do not have to confine yourself to just personal and professional confidence conditioning statements; imagine growth in any area of life you choose.

During performance, confidence conditioning statements become simplified statements for more memorable self-talk. The requirements for these statements are reduced to reflect the importance that they be present tense, positive, and emotional. All other requirements, however, continue to remain relevant. When you are getting ready to take the ice, use these confidence conditioning statements to maximize your positive mentality.

SAMPLE CONFIDENCE CONDITIONING STATEMENTS

1. I command confidence.

2. I trust in my abilities to execute one shift at a time.

3. Today is mine. I own this.

4. I am strong on my stick and make plays.

5. I love to set up and score goals.

6. Stay in control, baby – one-shift warrior!

7. I block all shots that come toward me.

8. I have a great first pass.

9. I get stronger, tougher, and sharper with each shift.

10. I am tough. I play hard every shift, I am a team player and I'm unstoppable. I am physically and mentally ready for every shift.

Whenever you read your confidence conditioning statements, pause and picture and feel them as you read them. Consciously use the self-talk voice within your head to create a video or picture of what it would look like to carry out your confidence conditioning statement in action.

Confidence is essential to the generation of a positive mentality. During competition, you must be confident in your ability to perform and trust that all your preparation will pay off. This practice of confidence conditioning not only helps you harness your self-talk voice, but it also builds internal confidence so that when the moment of truth arrives on the ice, you will believe in yourself and know that when all is said and done, you gave yourself the best chance for success. Thus, the process of building confidence will create the positive mentality necessary for success in your pursuit of excellence.

CAIN'S COACHING POINT:

What confidence conditioning statements, when read on a daily basis, will help you increase your confidence and increase your positive mentality?

_____

_____

_____

_____

_____

_____

_____

CAIN'S COACHING POINT:

Earlier in this manual we talked about your core values. How are you doing with living out those core values? Are you still setting weekly goals? Your chances for success significantly increase through the simple practice of setting daily goals. Remember, focus on the next 200 feet, working towards improvement and focusing on what you want, not what you are trying to avoid.

THE CONFIDENCE RESUME AND LIST OF WINS

Another strategy for creating a positive mentality and conditioning yourself to be more confident is to make a confidence resume and list of wins. The confidence resume and list of wins is an activity in which you identify all of the wins you have had in your career – wins both on and off the ice. The purpose of the confidence resume is to facilitate the development of greater confidence in yourself and your performance by listing all the qualifications that justify why you deserve the outcome you desire.

By nature, we as human beings beat ourselves up when we fall short of our goals and briefly celebrate our wins before we focus on what's next. For example, when you graduated from college, did you really enjoy and take confidence from the body of work you just completed, or were you focused on getting that first job out of school? When you were a child and learned how to ride a bike, did you take confidence from ditching the training wheels, or did you focus on going further and faster? Listing all of your wins will help you to see the amazing body of work you have done over time and will allow you to have a resource you can review to help build the mental muscle of confidence.

Your confidence resume and list of wins should include anything and everything that, when reviewed, helps you feel empowered and confident. The confidence resume and list of wins should be extensive and ongoing. Like climbing The Mountain of Hockey Excellence, the confidence resume and list of wins has no finish line. Your choices can focus on your personal, academic and athletic skills. They may include previous results, quality preparation, great teammates, books you have read, the people you have met, the places you have been, the wins you have had on the ice, the coaches you have played for, doing what was uncomfortable (asking someone out on a date) and celebrating that she said yes, or that you mustered up the courage to ask even though you were turned down (her mistake). Instead of focusing on the no, focus on the process that you asked. *Remember, you will never get anything in life that you don't ask for.*

CAIN'S COACHING POINT:

Get started with your confidence resume and list of wins. What are some of the wins you have had in your life that you may have overlooked?

_____

_____

_____

_____

_____

Filling out the confidence resume is beneficial for hockey players because it forces individuals to identify the work they've done and the preparation they've put into the development of their game. This exercise can provide the player with either a confidence boost or a look at a sobering reality. Even if the resume shows you have a lot of work to do, it is important to maintain a positive mentality by realizing you are on the right path and that the resume has given you the constructive criticism you need to get started on your journey. *Remember, it is the start that stops most people.*

CAIN'S COACHING POINT:

In my work with coaches and athletes, even the best athletes on the planet can struggle with developing their confidence resume. That struggle is exactly why we need to have the confidence resume in our arsenal as we climb The Mountain of Hockey Excellence. Confidence is fragile, and every time you review your confidence resume it will be the equivalent of lifting weights for your confidence and belief. You must do a little a lot to obtain the mental muscles you are looking for. Just as physical muscles take time and effort to develop, so do your mental muscles of confidence.

After you have written out your confidence resume and reasons to believe, post them where you will see them on a daily basis. I have my list on the nightstand next to my bed, and before I turn the lights out, I review my list and go to sleep feeling like a champion. Having this document visible will give you confidence by seeing you have reasons to believe in yourself. Some teams I work with will create a confidence resume for the season and review it before each game to remind the team of the hard work and preparation they have invested so that they should have confidence.

This daily and/or pre-game action is like strength and conditioning for your mental game. Through the repetitious acknowledgement of your reasons to be confident, you will steadily build a stronger, more confident mentality. During competition, this should be reason enough to stay positive while you embrace the adversity that hockey brings every day.

SOURCES OF CONFIDENCE

Confidence conditioning will improve positive self-talk, and the confidence resume will augment your belief in yourself and a positive mentality. Both techniques of confidence building rely on a solid base of preparation. True and authentic confidence comes from the combination of actions an individual takes in preparation for performance. Confidence comes from these four key areas:

1. Physical preparation – the BST (Blood, Sweat and Tears)

2. Positive self-talk & confidence conditioning

3. Performance routines you have to keep you consistent

4. Mental imagery of you performing at your best

There is no substitute for smart, hard work. The consistent implementation of effective mental conditioning with your physical conditioning will give you the biggest confidence boost. Physically, you would never do strength and conditioning once a week or once a semester and expect to get any stronger. The same rules apply to mental conditioning, and by integrating it into your physical conditioning, you get the most out of mind and body. Strengthening and conditioning to enhance your mental confidence is obtained by doing a little a lot, not a lot a little. Every time you grind it out in practice and give that extra effort, and every time you take the opportunity to reflect on your confidence conditioning statements and confidence resume, you build the mental muscle of confidence.

Conditioning self-confidence is all about building a positive mentality. When it comes down to your performance, all you can do is rely on your preparation and execute in a manner that gives you the best opportunity for success on that play. You cannot control anything else. You must strive for excellence in practices and games one play, one shift at a time to give yourself the peace of mind that you have done your best to give your best; the rest will fall into place.

KEEP YOUR CONFIDENCE HONEST

A great way to keep your confidence honest is through the utilization of an accountability partner(s). There are many different ways for teammates to keep each other accountable for building confidence. Feel free to arrange whatever methods you feel will serve you best in your program. One great way to keep your confidence honest is for your accountability partner to ask you questions about your confidence whenever you see each other. As teammates, if you see each other walking to class or in the dining hall, ask "Can you tell me two things on your confidence resume?" "What are three of your confidence conditioning statements?" If you do not respond within a few seconds, then you know you are not reviewing and giving enough focus to your mental conditioning techniques.

During practices, the question I ask players all the time is, "What are you working on today to get better?" If they cannot answer me quickly, they have not properly prepared for practice. They are not present and are not getting the most out of their time at practice that day. They are not building mental confidence and are not building a positive mentality necessary for performance excellence.

> "Preparation demands mental and physical conditioning and conscious planning. A player who is not ready and not totally prepared simply increases risk and is a liability to the team."
>
> *Jason Kersner*
> *Head Hockey Coach*
> *Skipjacks Hockey*

FAILURE IS POSITIVE FEEDBACK

In your pursuit of excellence, you will experience failure. This is a fact. Nothing worth having comes easy, and no self-made success story is created without trials and tribulations to overcome. Accept failure as an inevitable part of your journey and learn to view failure as positive feedback.

Failure is actually the most effective form of positive feedback. Failure provides you with the most direct and honest insight into why and how something has gone wrong. If you are trying to accomplish a task and are giving it your best effort, exercising various techniques but are failing, then you are receiving positive feedback from the task on what not to do. This is when you should become fascinated, not frustrated, and realize with each attempt you are exposing the details that will lead you to success.

Remember the prophecy of thoughts, and how your positive or negative thoughts manifest through actions and outcomes. Be positive. Be confident. **Confidence is a choice.** Challenge your limitations and move beyond your mistakes and shortcomings by learning from them. **In life there are winners and learners.** The quicker you make mistakes and learn from them, the quicker you move beyond them and the more prepared you are for the next 200 feet. Choose to be a learner, not a loser, and get better, not bitter. Accept failure as positive feedback.

CAIN'S COACHING POINT:

It is important to have the capacity to distinguish when you are getting closer to success and when you are moving further from it. Be sure to ask for advice or counsel when necessary, but be aware that this is your journey. Also, remember that sometimes when the accomplishment you desire feels far away, it actually may be waiting right around the corner.

THE THREE MAGIC LETTERS – YET

When you experience a disappointment in performance and the result you worked so hard to achieve falls beyond your reach, there is a three-letter word to keep your positive mentality – "YET." You can turn statements of failure into goal-setting exclamations by adding this simple three-letter word. This word will turn negative comments around and change your attitude, confidence and perspective. When you notice you are telling yourself (self-talk) that you cannot do this or that, add the three magic letters "Y-E-T" (#YET) to the end of your sentence.

I am not on the power play... YET.
I cannot score 30 goals... YET.
I do not squat 450... YET.
We didn't win the championship... YET.

By adding "YET" to the end of your sentence, you leave the door to your mental hall of excellence open as opposed to slamming the door in your own face. **YET is also an acronym for Your Energy Talks**, referring to the influence of your energy on yourself, your team and your goals. When the mood is down and thoughts are negative, use this acronym to remind yourself or others to change the outlook of the situation. Disappointments will occur in your performances, but treat failures as positive feedback and learning opportunities to work smarter and harder, and keep a positive mentality.

POSITIVE ENERGY IS CONTAGIOUS

Energy is contagious. Is yours worth catching?

People subconsciously take cues from others to gauge their own feelings. You probably know when your friends and teammates aren't feeling 100 percent even before they tell you, maybe even before they are aware of it. You definitely know when people are feeling great, because they often exude an aura of positivity that is difficult to ignore. Whether through an outward expression of body language or just feeling a vibe, humans are exceptional at interpreting moods. For better or worse, we are so proficient at detecting moods that we often subconsciously take direction from them and mimic that energy in our own actions. The importance of energy in performance should be quite clear.

If energy is contagious, it is obvious you should make that energy positive. **If you are a head coach reading this, your energy is THE MOST CONTAGIOUS**. Every team must decide to uphold the core covenant terms that represent the best of values – cooperation, hard work, and total concentration for the good of the team. The energy must come from you. You are the heart and soul of your team, and the energy you supply must be pumped out to all the extremities of your team.

Negative energy is simply counterproductive and detracts from gaining momentum for forward progress. A positive attitude when facing the challenges and obstacles of practice or competition goes a long way. Attitude reflects leadership, and if you perform with a positive attitude and bring positive energy on a daily basis, the atmosphere of your team and working environment will begin to reflect your commitment to positive energy. Therefore, if energy is contagious for producing attitudes and attitudes reflect leadership, then leadership, too, is contagious. As you perform, make a concerted effort to build a team of leaders by bringing positive energy to the table.

GET BIG

The term GET BIG refers directly to body language in relation to peak performance. It means to convey a big, confident body language. As you walk down the hall, on the floor of the weight room, on the ice or into your office, your body language is an expression of yourself and conveys a message to those around you.

What happens physiologically and psychologically as you GET BIG is that your brain and body will start to release chemicals that will make you feel more confident. You will start to come up with reasons why you should feel more confident, and you will become more confident. Psychology and physiology form a two-way street. You will affect your physical performance by how you think and talk to yourself, and you will affect your psychology by how you carry yourself physically, all the while reinforcing a positive self-image.

I have found that it is easier to act yourself into a way of thinking than it is to think yourself into a form of acting.

You must practice GETTING BIG by consciously walking BIG, and reinforce confidence by self-talking BIG. GETTING BIG will help you to find the confidence you need to perform at your best. One team I worked with that won an NCAA National Championship understands the importance of GETTING BIG and uses signs of success in their locker room to remind them of this key peak performance principle.

CAIN'S COACHING POINT:

Where will you hang a GET BIG sign where you can see it each day?

SELF-TALK – FINAL THOUGHTS

During performance, your "final thought" symbolizes the last conscious thought in your head before performing a specific action on that play. In the moment before you jump over the boards to start your shift, you want to narrow your mental focus on a word or phrase that mentally facilitates the physical accomplishment of that action. This final thought should reflect a positive mentality and affirm confidence to intensify your focus on the task at hand and thus increase the likelihood of its successful execution.

Too often athletes focus on what they want to avoid rather than what they want to accomplish. If the coach says, "play aggressive but don't take a penalty," "stop turning the puck over," "don't miss the net when you shoot," will you? **When the last thought you give an athlete is negative, negative things usually happen.**

If you use a negative statement at any point in the game, you have slammed the door of success. Rather, tell the player, "Brian, let's use the weak side of the ice on our breakouts" or "Brian, after you win the faceoff, let's establish a point shot." Call the players by name, positively reinforce what you want them to do, and then let them play.

Develop your own final thoughts for particular performance actions. Once you have chosen them, you want to incorporate these final thoughts into your performance routines to enhance the mind-body performance connection. Mentally conditioning a final thought will establish confidence by building a routine rhythm to your performance and time-out routine. Developing your own final thought process will undoubtedly help give you the best opportunity for performance excellence on each play.

CAIN'S COACHING POINT:

What are some final thoughts that you could use in your performance?

1) _____

2) _____

3) _____

REALISTIC POSITIVITY

A positive mentality alone will not grant you performance excellence. Do not get carried away with the thought that a positive mentality is the sole element of success, because positivity alone will get you nowhere – you must still take massive action. A positive mentality is, however, essential to the development of a present-moment focus on the process and play and your overall perception of performance and life. Positive people do better in the face of adversity, and hockey is a game of adversity.

CHAPTER #4 REVIEW

☐ Thoughts manifest through actions and affect outcomes.

☐ A positive mentality makes a significant difference between educational self-improvement and self-stagnation.

☐ Defeat limiting beliefs with a positive mentality.

☐ Keep a positive self-image.

☐ Self-talk is a reflection of self-image.

☐ Harness your self-talk through confidence conditioning.

☐ Your confidence conditioning statements build a positive mentality.

☐ Confidence resume facilitates development of confident performance.

☐ Keep your confidence honest by utilizing an accountability partner.

☐ Failure is positive feedback; get better, not bitter.

☐ Turn statements of failure into goal-setting exclamations by adding YET.

☐ YET – Your Energy Talks.

☐ Energy is contagious, so make yours positive.

☐ GET BIG with your body language and self-talk.

CHAPTER #5

CHAMPIONSHIP PREPARATION

> "Everybody wants to win. The will to win is worthless if you do not have the will to prepare. Separation is in preparation."
>
> **Brian Cain**
> **Peak Performance Coach**

In 2004, the California State University, Fullerton baseball team completed the first half of their season with a 15-16 record. At this midway point in the season, the team made the collective promise to turn their season around by placing their collective faith and trust in their preparation. In one of the greatest single-season turnarounds in college baseball history, Cal State Fullerton would go on to win the NCAA Division I National Championship with a final record of 47-22.

The Titans and their head coach George Horton were able to turn their season around with a commitment to the fundamentals and an intense focus on preparation, both physical and mental. I was a member of the Fullerton staff in 2002 and 2003, and I know firsthand that Coach Horton is a firm proponent of competing every day in practice as if it were a national championship game. I've seen firsthand how to replicate championship intensity in practice with proper structure and commitment to the preparation process.

When the team reached the College World Series in Omaha, Coach Horton brought a water bottle filled with dirt from the team's field in Fullerton. Before the start of the College World Series, the team went out onto the field and sprinkled that Fullerton dirt on the mound and in the batter's box of Rosenblatt Stadium, then the official home of the NCAA College World Series. This action served as a reminder to his players of all the hard work and preparation put in every day of practice back home, and that performance on the biggest stage of college baseball was no different than back home.

The game remains the same anywhere you play – nothing changes. It reminded players that the goal was to do the same thing in Omaha that they did every day in Fullerton – to continue to play against themselves and the game, throw quality pitches, have quality at-bats and play quality defense. It reminded the team that they compete as hard as anyone in the country on a daily basis in practice and that is what they were going to do in Omaha – nothing changes. It was clear that Horton and the Titans trusted their preparation, because the result took care of itself.

Although this is a baseball example, it could have just as easily been a hockey example. Playing one pitch at a time is no different than playing one shift at a time in hockey. Focusing on preparation and what you can control will give you the best chance for success on the diamond, on the ice and in life.

CHAMPIONSHIP PREPARATION

Preparation means everything to every team. As a player or a coach, you must make the proper mental and physical preparation prior to games. The light just doesn't come on when you hit the ice for warm-ups.

Players who claim they are "gamers" think that they are ready to play when they take the ice just before the opening faceoff. This is a huge mistake and shows the lack of discipline that it takes to be totally prepared for the contest at hand. Therefore, those players won't ever reach their potential because, as you've heard it said before, failure to prepare is preparing to fail. Preparation is the key to winning.

If you are a coach and your team is prepared poorly, then it has little chance of winning. A well-planned practice is an effective way to allow coaches to teach skills and fundamentals, cover offensive and defensive systems and tactics; but most of all, the players should be prepared in order to give them the confidence needed to play their best when it means the most.

Great coaches teach both the mental and physical preparation at practice. Great coaches give it to the players in segments so that they can grasp the concept. When a player makes a mistake or if you ask if he/she understands, then the answer usually is a nod of the head or a verbal "I know." Don't assume the player knows what to do. An example is to verbalize to your players three times what you expect them to do. This technique increases the chances that they will hear and remember what you just told them. If you expect execution in a game, then your players must practice that skill, power play, or defensive zone system for 21 days in order for it to start to become a habit. And you must reinforce the mental preparation the same way, all the time. You can't do it just once a week, twice a week, or sometimes. Mental preparation is just as important as physical preparation in being totally prepared to become a champion.

MENTAL PREPARATION

Mental preparation is fundamental to peak performance. In the words of John Wooden, "Nothing is better preparation for intense game pressure than countless hours of disciplined effort spent mastering the fundamentals." In this chapter, we focus on mastering the fundamentals of mental preparation through the implementation of effective mental conditioning practices and techniques.

Performance reflects preparation, and these strategies aim to cultivate a peak performance mentality as you practice for your performances, as well as the practices of your daily life. This chapter will help you establish a disciplined effort in developing a lifestyle of performance preparation.

GAME-LIKE PRACTICE

Game-like practice is essential for enhanced mental preparation. If you want to perform at a level of excellence, you must practice at a level of excellence. Practice is performance. The dictionary definition of "practice" is "to perform (an activity) or exercise (a skill) repeatedly or regularly in order to improve or maintain one's proficiency." This definition illustrates what peak performers must internalize: ***Repetition of quality performance is fundamental to the achievement of excellence in hockey, in life.***

Coaches are always telling players that "You will play like you practice, so you should practice like you play." This is contingent, however, on making practices game-like. The purpose of game-like simulations is to help familiarize players with the conditions they will face in the heat of competition. Repeated exposure to game-like conditions is the best method to mentally condition for the real game. When your time comes to perform on the big stage, if you already put in the hard work to accustom yourself to the environment, it will pay off through your performance.

PRACTICE: PRE-GAME TO POST-GAME

In order to be totally prepared for games, great hockey coaches will also practice time-outs, the national anthem and where they will meet in the locker room for pre-game and between-period preparations.

One of your team's goals should be to out-prepare every opposing team on your schedule. The attitude of your team should be that practices are not to prepare for a rival opponent or a tournament game but to develop the potential of the team and to play their best when it means the most, which is every day. Championship teams display excellent work ethic in practice. A successful team will have a great work ethic. The teams that are successful will prepare hard every day, and when they have success, then they can trace their performance back to preparation. A great coach only focuses on the controllable factors. The amount of preparation is one aspect of hockey over which each coach has complete control. When you control what you can control, then you will become more successful.

REWARDED BEHAVIOR = REPEATED BEHAVIOR

Developmental psychology espouses that rewarded behavior becomes repeated behavior, true for both poor and quality behavior. By rewarding specific steps in the preparation process when executed properly, the development of skill proficiency is enhanced. Coupled with simulated competition in game-like practices, players place themselves in the best environment to cultivate performance excellence.

What a player wants to hear most is his or her name attached to a specific positive compliment. As you pass out praise to your teammates, the more specific you can be, the more beneficial the impact of that praise. Telling Brian that he did a good job means very little because Brian does not hear exactly what he did to receive the positive compliment. But telling Brian that he did a great job backchecking all the way into our defensive zone, after a sustained offensive shift that generated a scoring chance, rewards him for his pursuit of excellence on the rink. Through this positive reinforcement, rewarding proficiency will ultimately improve performance.

STRATEGIES FOR GAME-LIKE PRACTICE

1. **MAKE IT COMPETITIVE** – have both a winner and loser for everything. If there is a winner and a loser when you play in competition, structure that same competitiveness within your daily practices so that everything you do simulates that competitive intensity. Athletes love competition, so giving athletes more opportunities to compete will increase intensity and enhance development. Giving each player an individual win/loss record for competitions held each day and then posting these win/loss records so that they can be seen each day help to show who the best competitors and best winners are in your program. Competing against each other sets standards of excellence in practice that will help take your practice competitiveness to the next level.

2. **DIFFERENT-COLORED JERSEYS** will help create a separation between the two teams and give the practice a more competitive flavor. Often, using just two jersey colors is better than having a different color for each line combination. The game is played with two different jerseys, so practice should be as well. Drills/small-area games that coaches can use with two jersey colors and one puck best simulate game day. When you put the practice jersey on, it becomes part of your routine and helps an athlete's segmentation from school (boy/girl scout mentality) into hockey player (bounty hunter mentality). Athletes also appear more uniform when in uniform, which seems only appropriate. This emphasizes the importance of the team as a unit, setting the stage for the collective "we" over the individual "me."

If you can break out your game jersey, this is a great opportunity for the players to see if the jerseys fit comfortably and do not hinder any physical movements. It also helps create that competitive environment of two teams going head-to-head to enhance competition.

3. **BRING IN OFFICIALS WHEN YOU SCRIMMAGE**: This will free up coaches and athletes on your team from having to make the calls. It will also increase the competitive nature of the scrimmage because it is more game-like.

4. **USE A SCOREBOARD** so that the coaches and athletes can keep track of the stats just as you would in competition. Creating a process-based scoring system in which you give points for specific aspects of performance is also a great way to reward the behavior you want in your team. For example, giving two points to the team whose player finishes a check in the scrimmage will reward the type of behavior desired in games. It will also give instant feedback to the team that playing hard with great effort is sometimes worth as much as a scoring play.

PROCESS-BASED SCORING SYSTEM

A strategy to make practice more game-like is to create a process-based scoring system for intra-squad scrimmages. Under the premise that rewarded behavior becomes repeated behavior, points are earned for a player's effort and execution of particular skills rather than just points for scoring a goal.

Coaches often choose to use process-based scoring systems during practice to highlight particular skills in which the team must improve. I often recommend coaches begin using this system to focus on one particular skill at a time. As players familiarize themselves with the framework of the system that the coach has implemented, the coach may introduce and highlight more skills to monitor. This process-based scoring system is, like all systems of preparation, one of steady progression. Coaches may even add different dimensions to the scoring system, such as taking away points or giving points to the other team for anything seen as disrespect in the game.

Below is an example of a process-based scoring system for hockey:

DEFENSIVE

BLOCKED SHOT +1pt

FINISHED CHECK +1pt

TAKEAWAY +1pt

STICK PENALTY -1pt

OFFENSIVE

SCORING CHANCE FOR +1pt

REBOUND SHOT +1pt

GOAL OR ASSIST +1pt

DRAWN PENALTY +1pt

TEAM

GREY ZONE TURNOVER -1pt

OFFSIDES OR ICING -1pt

DROPPED STICK -1pt

CAIN'S COACHING POINT:

The process-based scoring system can be changed to fit your program needs, and you can award points for any part of the process that you wish to emphasize.

I've seen these process-based scoring systems implemented to encourage performance excellence in everything a team does during preparation. If there is a non-hustle play, two points go on the board for the other team. If there is team energy with involvement, such as players getting excited for blocking a shot, they get two points on the scoreboard for energy and engagement, because energy and engagement are two very important parts of the process of playing championship hockey.

EXTRA EFFORTS OF EXCELLENCE

To further emphasize the significance of excellent preparation in all things, no matter how small, let's explore the importance of extra efforts. By elaborating on the importance of the aforementioned example of being ourselves on the ice and at practice, the crossover effect from preparation to competitive performance becomes clear. For example, a teammate may look at other players and say they are excellent but they may feel they are not. Every player has the ability to be excellent, but one player may be a better skater or scorer.

Every team has this situation each year. However, a player may be very responsible defensively, finish his checks and block shots. This player is an example of extra effort. The player who finds his or her role and plays to excellence is contributing to the best of the team. Extra effort from one player can help raise you to the next level and provide the enthusiasm that can make your team champions.

PRACTICE MAKES PERMANENT

Practice does not make perfect; practice makes permanent. It is the quality of your practice that gives you the best chance for quality performance. If your practice is high or low quality, you can be certain your performance will reflect it. Also, notice that I am highlighting quality instead of quantity. I mentioned the value of quality repetition earlier, and it cannot be overemphasized. You can practice something all day long, but if you have practiced the wrong technique, all that preparation means little. ***Working hard at the wrong thing does not work.*** It is not the quantity, but the quality that counts. This is also why proper mental conditioning is so significant, because if you do not exercise a winning mentality, you are bound to lose.

It is your obligation in your pursuit of excellence to utilize your preparation time to make the right skills permanent. As athletes, we do not often, if ever, have control over the situations in competition. In practice, however, the control is ours. In practice, you control the repetition of rehearsing plays and running through game-like scenarios. In practice, you can try something over and over again. Take advantage of that time, because we all know that when game time rolls around and the stakes are elevated, you only have one shot to get it right. This is also why elevating the level of practice to simulate game-like intensity is beneficial. Recognize that practice makes permanent; control the quality of preparation – it will determine how you perform.

PAY ATTENTION TO DETAIL

The practice of mental preparation is founded on attention to detail. When you give the little details the same treatment as the larger ones, you give yourself the most opportunities to employ techniques of the mental game. **Excellence in small things is excellence in all things.**

This applies not only to when you practice your sport, but to cultivating your mental preparation through daily actions representative of that preparation mentality. With the adoption of this lifestyle, the practice of mental conditioning becomes routine and this perspective becomes habit. Daily tasks become performance preparation. All the more reason to seize the day, and take PRIDE (Personal Responsibility In Daily Excellence) in your preparation.

HAVE YOU EVER BEEN BIT BY AN ELEPHANT?

Have you ever been bitten by an elephant? What about a mosquito? My guess is that you have never been bitten by an elephant but have been bitten by plenty of mosquitoes. Please understand that hockey and life are the same way. It is the little things that add up over time. It is not the BIG elephants that keep us from achieving excellence; it is the small daily decisions, the metaphorical mosquito bites that either take us where we want to go or hold us back.

PERFORMANCE INTENSITY

If you want to improve your performance in games, the best way to begin is to start increasing the intensity of your practices. This can be accomplished by increasing the tempo and pace in practice. The harder and faster you compete in practice, the more comfortable you feel in games. Award-winning author Jon Gordon wrote in his book *Training Camp: "What greatness really requires is a willingness to be uncomfortable. Here's the deal. If you are always striving to get better, then you are always growing. And if you are growing, then you are not comfortable. To be the best, you have to be willing to be uncomfortable and embrace it as part of your growth process."* **You must learn in practice to get comfortable with being uncomfortable.**

If you can make decisions and actions happen faster in practice than in games, you are giving yourself the best chance to play at your best against teams or players who have more talent. When you face these opponents, the pace of the game tends to speed up. If you practice under up-tempo conditions, you will be more capable of holding your own, because you will have established – mentally and physically – the endurance and stamina through your preparation.

Remember, tempo and pace are measured under time. Find ways you can use a stopwatch in practice to pick up the pace of play and make your pace of play faster than it will be on game night.

BE QUICK, BUT DO NOT HURRY

One of Coach Wooden's great maxims was the advice, "Be quick, but do not hurry." This is significant because you want to increase the tempo of practice without compromising the quality of the practice. This is an important balancing act in your performance preparation. If you work too fast, the more mistakes you will make and the less you improve your game. This rule is applicable to the development of both physical skills and mental skills.

Coach Wooden's advice, however, serves as a warning to those who want to shortcut the process. Before you increase the intensity of performance, you should be proficient in the fundamental skills necessary for such performance. This seems intuitive, but when people hurry to play at the highest level, they often run headfirst into the brick wall of reality – the reality that there is no shortcut to excellence. This is why it is important to make sure to practice technique before you increase tempo. It is good to be a quick study, but some things should not be rushed. Sometimes the best way to learn something is to take care and be methodical, and then steadily increase the pace of your practice.

In order to prepare for performance, you should push the pace in practice and make yourself uncomfortable. *It is absolutely necessary to learn how to be comfortable with being uncomfortable* if you want to perform at a level of excellence. *Growth happens on the edge of discomfort.* It is important to practice a fast pace and quick tempo, but do not hurry your preparation.

THE "STEP UP" HAPPENS EVERY DAY

A lot of athletes say they will "step up their game" when they play their division rivals or that they will "step it up" in the big game. As a peak performance coach, this is both perplexing and insightful. It is perplexing because if you have the ability to "step up," why are you not "stepping up" at today's practice? It is simultaneously insightful because it shows the mentality of the player(s) saying this, illustrating an immature perspective towards performance. These players obviously do not understand the value of excellent preparation.

There is no "step up." If you can play at the highest level by stepping up, the step up must occur every day so that there is no step up. There is no conceivable reason to not play at your best during competition; there isn't even a conceivable reason to not do it in practice. As Michael Jordan said, "I play to win, whether during practice or a real game, and I will not let anything get in the way of me and my competitive enthusiasm to win." Jordan would probably ask, why "step up" in the big game when it is what you should be doing every day in practice?

As we have discussed, performance reflects preparation. You will not maximize your potential if you pursue excellence only once in a while during practice sessions. If you wish to be a success, you must pursue excellence all the time. The "step up" happens every day. *Excellence is a lifestyle, not an event.*

MEASUREMENT = MOTIVATION

Kevin Sneddon, the head hockey coach at The University of Vermont, implemented mental conditioning as the foundation of his program. One of the keys to Coach Sneddon's success with his teams was his understanding that measurement equals motivation.

One of the best ways to motivate yourself is to measure your progress. Simply believing that you will give your best without specific measurement of performance is unrealistic. Coach Sneddon recognized this and, with his attention to detail, he measured all the preparation of his team to motivate his players and to instill mental conditioning techniques. His simple utilization of a scoreboard is all it takes.

Coach Sneddon would keep stats during drills and post the results the next day so everyone on the team could see how they compared to their teammates. Naturally, as competitors, they wanted to get on the top of the list. Coach Sneddon gives his team measurements to gauge their daily efforts compared to their best scores on record in specific drills that they do on a frequent basis. In doing so, players on the team are held accountable for their efforts in their daily preparation, which makes the whole team practice harder and at a higher level on a consistent basis.

THE POWER OF TIME

During preparation, a stopwatch, scoreboard or video camera is a great accountability partner for a peak performer. They are simple to use, unbiased, and blatantly honest about your performance effort. As the last section espoused, measurement equals motivation, and time is one of the great motivators in life. The utilization of a stopwatch is sure to motivate you to constantly improve your times, wherever appropriate, during your preparation routines.

The use of a stopwatch anywhere, from lifting weights to simulating competitive game-time scenarios, will draw the excellence out of your performance. By pressuring players to accomplish game-like scenarios in a limited amount of time, if not a shorter time than during competition, they will learn to cope with uncomfortable situations. This can be applied to hockey by giving your power play unit only 30 seconds to score a goal, or by timing a drill where your forwards attack the net on a line rush but then have to transition to defense and backcheck. These examples can help force increased efficiency and speed of getting up and down the rink in game-like conditions. Ultimately, this forces players to work faster than they normally would if there were no stopwatch, and as fast or faster than they will need to be in a game.

Utilizing a stopwatch in your performance preparation will immediately increase the game-like speed, intensity, and tempo while you practice. You will also learn to cope with pressure and feel comfortable with uncomfortable situations, because on the edge of discomfort is where learning takes place.

Think about how you can implement a stopwatch in your preparation to help create an environment of pressure and discomfort to enhance your performance development. By keeping track of time and pushing yourself, the game will reward you for your efforts in your competitive performance.

CAIN'S COACHING POINT:

What can you measure to make your preparation process more competitive and to make you work faster than you might have to in a game?

1)_____

2)_____

3)_____

RECORD PROGRESS

One of the most effective methods to measure performance improvement is to regularly record your progress in your copy of *Brian Cain's Peak Performance Journal.* When athletes take the initiative to record the details of their progress in a journal of some kind, they hold themselves accountable for their preparation. Such a journal can be used to keep quantifiable measurements of preparation drills, to help remove the emotions from daily preparation and to record factual assessments. Journaling can also be used to record reflections of daily performance, helping to understand how your feelings that day impacted your performance.

For each day of performance preparation, write down times, important lessons, areas in need of improvement, a goal for the next day based off today's practice session, and anything else that applies to your performance. Recording progress grants the opportunity to apply the three steps of performance improvement. It enables you to reflect on the information you record, generates awareness of areas of improvement, and enables you to create and implement new strategies for performance development. When you know what giving your best is and it is on record, you can better judge your effort with objectivity. This speeds up the learning and the improvement process. In sum, when you record progress, you make record progress.

HOW TO KEEP A PEAK PERFORMANCE HOCKEY JOURNAL

One of the most beneficial routine exercises someone in the pursuit of excellence can do is keep a peak performance journal. The peak performance journal is a tool to help you further develop your mental skills for optimal performance. Remember, you must be in control of yourself before you can control your performance. The first step in gaining self-control is to develop an awareness of your performance, so that you can recognize when you are distracted from the present moment and the most appropriate mental state for success.

DEVELOP AWARENESS

Developing awareness is the first step towards consistent levels of performance. Remember the three steps to performance change: (1) Awareness, (2) Strategy, (3) Implementation of the strategy. This journal provides you with an opportunity to record the different strategies you are working on to maintain and regain self-control.

GET IT OUT OF YOUR HEAD AND ON PAPER

The long-range goal is to develop various strategies you can implement in stressful situations to help you perform at your best when it means the most. If you choose to, the journal also can be a place where you can record your feelings and the personal knowledge that you are gaining about yourself, the game, your teammates, and any other factors. This is one of the few times in your life that you will ever direct so much energy toward one specific goal. There is a lot to learn from your pursuit of excellence. This journal will give you something to reflect on after your high-level participation is completed.

The journal also can serve as a place where you can express your feelings in writing or drawings. It is beneficial to get these feelings out in some way so that they do not build up and lead to unproductive tension. The use of colored pens is often helpful to express yourself, even if you are not an artist. Research has shown this strategy to be a beneficial stress management technique.

CREATE A ROUTINE FOR WRITING

You do not have to make an entry every day, but should strive to be consistent in your writing routine. *Remember, to be consistently successful you must be able to describe what you do as a process/routine.* Make your journal entries as routine as possible by writing at the same time of day or in the same place, such as your locker, at your desk or in your bed at home.

The journal is an informal record of your thoughts and experiences as you train for high-level performance. If you choose to have someone read your journal, please feel free to delete or cover up any parts that you think are too personal to share. The objective for someone who is reviewing your writing should be to guide you and to make suggestions that may facilitate your self-exploration in reaching your goals.

I highly recommend that you try the peak performance hockey journal as a strategy to learn about yourself and speed up your learning curve. Remember, it's the start that stops most people, so commit to it for the next 2-3 weeks and feel free to write whatever comes to your mind. The following section includes suggestions with accompanying questions/descriptors that can help guide your entries. As with all things, you will become more comfortable with the journal process as you develop a routine over time.

SAMPLE QUESTIONS TO WRITE ABOUT

1. **PEAK PERFORMANCE:** What does it feel like when you play and/or practice at your best? Describe some of your most enjoyable experiences playing hockey. What have you learned from these moments when you are playing at your best?

2. **STRESSORS:** Write down your thoughts about various events outside hockey that are distracting to you. For example, parents, girlfriends, peers, job hassles, financial issues, community (hometown expectations). Do the same for distractions on the ice, such as importance of contest, location, spectators, etc.

3. **COACHING STYLE:** What do you need from your coaches? How can you best help them help you reach your goals? What can you do to make your relationship with your coaches more productive?

4. **TEAMMATES:** What do you want from your teammates? What can you give them? How do you relate and work with your teammates? Write about your relationship with other teammates. Any unfinished business you need to work through?

5. **CONFIDENCE:** At this time, how confident are you in regard to achieving your goals? What can you do differently to act more confidently? What can you ask of yourself, coach and/or teammates?

6. **MANIFESTATIONS OF YOUR STRESS:** How do you experience high levels of anxiety in performance? Assess your thoughts, physiological and behavioral reactions. What strategies did you use to help intervene with your stress and keep balance?

7. **AWARENESS AND CONCENTRATION:** What changes do you observe in your performance when you are aware? What concentration methods are you experimenting with? What are your ABC's or focal points for various skills?

TRUST YOUR PREPARATION

Hockey is the ultimate game of preparation – and that doesn't even take off-season workouts, meetings, film sessions and in-season workouts into consideration! Most hockey games are won or lost before the first practice even takes place in the fall!

Therefore, preparation is everything to a hockey player. It is taking all the elements necessary for performance excellence and practicing them tirelessly and with a relentless energy to achieve progress. As you read through this book, integrate all the material into your preparation.

The constant practice of mental conditioning with your physical conditioning is of utmost significance to reaching the pinnacle of performance excellence. As the great master of preparation, Coach John Wooden, used to say, **"Failing to prepare is preparing to fail."**

Most importantly, trust your preparation. Placing trust in your performance preparation and taking pride in the fact that you are doing things the right way will make all the difference in your journey. The climb up The Mountain of Hockey Excellence will undoubtedly be treacherous at times, but if you trust that you have prepared at a consistent effort of excellence, your preparation is bound to reward you.

CHAPTER #5 REVIEW

☐ Repetition alone does not bring rewards; it is the quality that matters.

☐ Rewarded behavior becomes repeated behavior.

☐ Make practices competitive.

☐ Utilize a process-based scoring system to reward desired performance.

☐ Extra efforts give you the competitive advantage.

☐ Practice does not make perfect; practice makes permanent.

☐ Attention to details makes the difference.

☐ "Be quick, but do not hurry."

Coach John Wooden

☐ You must learn to be comfortable with being uncomfortable.

☐ The "step up" happens every day.

☐ Measurement equals motivation; you treasure what you measure.

☐ A stopwatch is a great motivator and accountability partner.

☐ When you record progress, you make record progress.

☐ "Failing to prepare is preparing to fail."

Coach John Wooden

CHAPTER #6

PERFORMANCE ROUTINES
HOW YOU PLAY ONE SHIFT
AT A TIME

> "We are what we repeatedly do. Excellence, then, is not an act, but a habit."
>
> **Aristotle**

The secrets of success are hidden in the routines of our daily lives. You can know all the information within the previous chapters, but if you do not implement this information, then what good does it do for you? The purpose of any routine is to build more trust and consistency in performance.

Routines are effective because they give structure by providing a consistent starting point to activate a regular procedure. In hockey, a consistent frame of reference is essential to performance excellence by providing the mind and body a sense of security even under conditions that remain out of your control. The familiarity of routines establishes good performance habits, and your investment in cultivating them will pay big dividends on your pursuit of excellence.

This chapter will explore routines that will implement the information you learned in the previous chapters. We will discuss routines that keep you in the present moment and focused on the process of playing one shift at a time; routines that give you the necessary perspective to maintain a positive mentality; and routines to establish during your preparation, placing you in a position to give yourself the best chance for success.

PRE-GAME & POST-GAME ROUTINES

Pre-game and post-game routines are important for all coaches and players to develop. The purpose of these routines is to transform your mentality from your "real self" (boy/girl scout) to your "performing self" (bounty hunter) and vice versa.

Most players have pre-game routines. Some individual pre-game routines I've witnessed range from players listening to a particular song or playlist, putting on their uniforms in a particular order, doing a certain set of stretches, and leaving the team to do mental imagery in silence for a couple minutes by themselves. Teams also have routines they follow before going out to perform in games, whether they are team warm-ups, team meetings/huddles, or team chants to bring up the energy levels. The purpose of these routines is to make you feel comfortable by giving you a sense of familiarity, which brings confidence, while transforming you into your competitive mentality.

Pre-game rituals are even more important to individuals and teams when you have to go on the road and play in an unfamiliar environment. While working with a girls high school team on the mental game, I attended one of their games in the state playoffs. The girls were the visiting team and politely asked if everyone could leave the dressing room prior to taking the ice. The team then proceeded to turn off the light in the locker room and began a series of responsive chants while in total darkness. I asked the coach what that was about, and he told me that they came up with it and did it before every game; it got them focused so he allowed them to do it. **The girls' routine helped his players find comfort in an uncomfortable environment.**

Post-game routines are a system of steps that allow the coaches and players to decompress after competition. Most players' post-game routines consist of having a brief post-game meeting with their coach or team, taking off their uniforms, cleaning themselves up, getting dressed, and calling it a day. Post-game routines, however, have the potential to be much more significant than this process of "going through the motions." Later in this chapter you'll learn how to create a post-game routine that enhances your pursuit of post-performance excellence so that you can extract as much learning as possible from each experience.

IN-GAME ROUTINES

An in-game routine provides the player and coach with a set of mental checkpoints. By going through a series of mental checkpoints, athletes place themselves in the present moment and focus on the process at hand. In the heat of competition, these routines serve as a chance for athletes to control themselves and their performances.

CAIN'S COACHING POINT:

The most important part of your in-game routine in hockey is that you take a deep breath. Taking a deep breath before your shift as a part of your in-game routine helps you to separate this play/shift from other plays/shifts; it keeps you in the moment and in control of yourself.

Make sure that your coaches and teammates are aware of your in-game routines. This is important because they can act as accountability partners during performance and can remind you to check back into your routines if you are in a funk. You should also learn the in-game routines of your teammates so you can return their focus on a familiar frame of reference. In-game routines are imperative to self-control, giving you the best opportunity to execute with performance excellence.

CIRCLE OF FOCUS

Inside of your in-competition routine, you step into your circle of focus. The circle of focus is an imaginary circle that you step into and engage in a present-moment focus with your energy and attention going out towards the action taking place. For example, the players step into their circle of focus after a whistle right before the next faceoff or on the bench just after the coach calls the next lineup and before your shift starts. Since hockey is such a dynamic game, players have to maintain certain checkpoints during the game to transpire from offense to defense while stepping into this metaphorical circle of focus. It is a critical part of the in-competition routine in which you get into the present moment and play one shift at a time.

As part of the in-competition routine, you want to use one to three mental strategies to keep your focus locked into the present.

1. Deep breath on a focal point

2. Visualization/mental imagery of execution of the play

3. Verbalize – self-talk of final thought/ABC's

CAIN'S COACHING POINT:

Because we cannot see if the athletes are doing mental imagery and we cannot see if they are using their final thoughts, as coaches, we want our players to take a deep breath each play so we can see that they are in control of themselves.

These strategies will assist your focus on performing in the present moment. Routine use of one or more of the strategies will help you enter that circle of focus and gain control of your mind. Mind control leads to body control, which leads to skill/performance control, and being in control of all aspects of yourself gives you the best chance for performance excellence.

VERBALIZING YOUR FINAL THOUGHT

We have discussed how athletes use self-talk during performance, and an athlete's final thought builds upon the self-talk concept in a more play-specific manner. As discussed earlier, the final thought is the last thought in an athlete's mind before performing a specific aspect of the game. Before making a play, you want to think to yourself a particular positive phrase that intensifies your focus on the accomplishment of that play. You want to integrate this final thought into your performance routine to strengthen the mind-body performance connection. Mentally conditioning a final thought will establish a routine rhythm to your performance, giving you the best opportunity for performance excellence on a consistent shift-by-shift basis.

There is a significant difference between being on the ice or going over the boards and telling yourself to "take the body, be aggressive" and telling yourself "don't play soft." Your final thought will make a big difference in your performance because a positive and aggressive final thought will give you the best chance to follow through in your performance.

DRILLS FOR FINAL THOUGHTS

Practicing final thoughts is important to maximize their effectiveness on a routine basis. When working with hockey teams, I set up a basic drill for each position group and have the players verbalize their final fundamental thoughts out loud. I ask the players to say their final thought aloud just before beginning their rep, and I listen as well as watch the physical execution of the drill. Out loud, they are saying their final thoughts such as "head up!" or "tape to tape" or "head on a swivel." We take three reps with the verbalization of the final thought so that I can hear what their final thought is. ***Their final thought is always one of their ABC's for performance as mentioned earlier in this book.***

Peak performers also utilize mental imagery as a component of their performance routines. The use of mental imagery is an excellent way to psychologically prepare yourself for performance by visualizing yourself executing a specific task within your sport.

SUPERMAN SEGMENTATION AND SEPARATION

Segmentation routines are used to help separate yourself from the many different activities you have. If you are reading this and you are a college or high school athlete, you have school, social activities, and sport to separate in your life; if you are a professional, you have at least the latter two. Inside of those different aspects of your life, you may need to take care of a family member, work a job, spend time with your significant other and friends, etc. One of the best techniques to help segment and separate the many activities you have is to use something physical (perhaps entering the locker room) to help you change your mental state. It is here we look to Superman for guidance.

Superman is the ultimate pro at segmentation and separation prior to and after his performances. He walks into the phone booth as Clark Kent, super nerd (student), and comes out as Superman (hockey player and one-shift warrior), superhero. His self-transformative process is the perfect example for peak performance segmentation routines. The nearest phone booth is the symbolic equivalent of his locker room: As he changes his clothes, his perspective changes, as he adopts a peak performance mentality.

One hockey team I worked with took this principle so far as to get a Superman logo for the outside of their locker room door to serve as a reminder that when you walked into the locker room to change your clothes, you were also changing your mentality from student (Clark Kent) to athlete (Superman).

As you take off each item of your street clothes and put on your hockey equipment or T-shirt and shorts for a workout, think about the transformation taking place and the necessary change in mentality. Release the mental bricks from your personal life as you get into your performance mentality, or release the mental bricks of your performance after practice as you return yourself to your personal life. Changing your clothes is a process to help you separate the mentality you need to succeed in the various segments of your life, by breaking down the process into various segments. The establishment of these routines gives you the best chance to be in the present for whatever you are about to perform, and to have a consistent mentality to be where you need to be when you need to be there.

MOVE THROUGH THE HOURGLASS

Another way to think about the process of routines, segmentation and separation is to imagine an hourglass as a visual example of how your pre-performance and post-performance routines will work. The shape of the hourglass reflects the segmentation and separation process, with a definite start point (top of the hourglass) and end point (bottom of the hourglass) with a defined middle section.

This hourglass shape mirrors the self-transformative routine because you begin the process as either your "real self" or "performing self" and end as the opposite. The hourglass transformation is marked by some physical routine actions such as changing clothes, where you strip down from your school clothes to your team uniform. When you are naked during the process of changing, you are in the middle of that transformative process – the middle of the hourglass.

Changing your clothes is common routine for segmentation and separation; but a number of other routines, such as turning off the cell phone, putting on your skates, or taking a shower, can also mark the self-transformation.

CAIN'S COACHING POINT:

I suggest using your cell phone as a tool to help you transform yourself and as a reminder to stay in the present moment. When you turn off your cell phone, it is a sign that you are shifting your mentality from student to athlete, and that you are letting go of the academics, social media, significant other, friends, family and other potential distractions that could keep you from being the ultimate athlete. When you turn off that cell phone, you are going to feel yourself moving through your mental hourglass and becoming a peak performer.

The athletes I work with hardly ever turn their cell phones off, so when they do, that means they are going to be doing something special. You have got to treat practice and games like they are special opportunities for development, because they are. Let nothing outside of your sport interfere with mentally preparing for performance.

CAIN'S COACHING POINT:

If you are a coach, I suggest you get practice jerseys and/or workout apparel for your team, something as simple as the same T-shirt and/or shorts. This will help your athletes with the segmentation process as they change into a uniform. You will teach them the importance of the mindset that they need to have when that uniform is on. Invest the time to educate them on the importance of changing the clothes and changing the mindset to get present.

After you turn your cell phone off, you then start the process of changing your clothes. As you take off your shirt, let go of the test you failed. As you take off your pants, let go of the person who cut you off on your drive into practice. As you take off your shoes, there go the issues you are having at home. As you physically change your clothes, you are ridding yourself of all that mental baggage and turning yourself into the ultimate athlete. As you move toward the middle of the hourglass, you become fully present and fully focused on what you plan to accomplish today at practice.

Then, as you put on your performance gear, you feel yourself getting more energized and more focused. As you lace up your skates, you feel locked in and prepared to perform to the best of your abilities, striving for performance excellence. Finally, you come out on the other end of the hourglass, mentally prepared to DOMINATE THE DAY! By following this hourglass segmentation and separation routine, you set the stage for a quality performance.

BORDER RULE

David Dubois was the former head hockey coach at North Country Union High School. During his tenure, Dubois' teams were known for playing physical, fast-paced and up-tempo. He developed what he called his "Border Rule." He instructed his players that when they crossed the border of the locker room door and went out into the arena the only thing that mattered was hockey. He coached his players to use the border as the last bit of their routine to help segment between their student/social self (real self) and their hockey self (performing self). What is your metaphorical border?

WHEN IS THE GLADIATOR READY FOR BATTLE?

The last thing you do before performance should be part of a physical routine to signal you are ready to perform. One of the best illustrations of this is in the movie *Gladiator,* when Maximus (Russell Crowe) reaches down for a bit of earth to rub between his hands and then throws the remnants back to the ground. This is his pre-game routine symbolizing he has gathered his battle mentality. It is a sign that Maximus is in the present moment, nothing can distract his focus, and he is ready to perform in war.

Develop your own pre-game routine to collect your performance mentality. I often suggest that you take a moment and retie your skates to check into your performance state of mind. By doing this, you lace it up and lock it in. NHL Hall of Famer Nicklas Lidstrom is famous for his pre-game preparations and routines – from his meals, to time he arrives at rink, the path he walks into the locker room, to his physical preparation. Whatever the physical act may be, use it to activate your performance mentality and enter your circle of focus. Let yourself know that you are Gladiator ready and going to battle on the ice as a one-shift warrior.

FOCAL POINTS, DEEP BREATHS, SELF-CONTROL

Whenever you perform, it is important to have and utilize focal points. Focal points are mental checkpoints that you go to throughout your journey up The Mountain of Hockey Excellence as a part of your in-competition routine. You check in on your mental and emotional state and, when necessary, bring yourself back into the present moment. Hockey players could use a spot on the scoreboard or somewhere on the bench as a focal point that they go to and take a deep breath between shifts or when the game starts to speed up on them. Another team I work with, the Skipjacks, gives players a green sticker and players use that as their focal point. This technique allows players to have a routine in which they are able to look at their focal point, take a deep breath and get back to a calm, focused and centered place in the present moment ready for the next shift. ***Remember, you must be in control of yourself before you can control your performance, and the #1 way to get control of yourself is to take a deep breath.***

The routine use of a focal point and a deep breath will put you in control of yourself and in a better place mentally and physically, giving you the best chance for success.

CAIN'S COACHING POINT:

What is a focal point you can use at your practice rink or on your equipment to help you regain control?

_____

_____

TAKE A DEEP BREATH

The deep breath is an important part of any performance routine, because the breath connects you to the present moment. Taking a deep breath pulls you right back to the "here" and the "now." The deep breath brings oxygen into your system, slows down your heart rate, clears your mental state and puts you back in control of yourself.

CAIN'S COACHING POINT:

When as a part of your in-game routine can you take a deep breath?

_____

_____

As a hockey coach, you want to see your players breathe between each shift so that you have a visual reference point to identify where they are mentally at each play. Having them take a deep breath enables you as the coach to recognize when players are letting the game speed up on them and if they are working a process to help them settle back down and stay in control of their emotions. In pressure situations, often the first thing to break down will be the player's routine. Once a player loses his or her routine, next goes mind control, then physical performance. Make sure to take your deep breaths during performance to keep your head in YOUR game.

ROUTINE PERFORMANCE REVIEW

A routine review of your most recent performance is one of the best post-game routines you can establish on your pursuit of performance excellence. Keeping a peak performance journal chronicles your progress and development in your mental and physical conditioning, providing you with a valuable resource for self-improvement. This gives you the ability to reflect upon past performances and recall how you performed, how you were feeling, what you believe you need to improve, what performance adjustments you must make, whether or not past performance adjustments worked, etc. In the previous chapter I addressed how recorded progress becomes record progress, and making the act of recording performances a routine is the first step in the right direction.

The best time to integrate this performance routine review is directly after performance, while it is fresh in your mind. Record all the information about your performance that is applicable to future improvement. As you push yourself to excellence, challenge yourself to become better by being self-critical and not being merely content with a solid performance. Make sure, however, that you also give some focus to what you did well. Doing this will serve as a reminder to you to continue performing these aspects of the game and will enable you to catch yourself if those aspects of your game start slipping. This is all invaluable information for developing your performance to become a peak performer in hockey.

MAKE IT ROUTINE

A routine is a skill that needs to be practiced regularly so that it becomes, well, routine. You cannot just do a routine once and expect to have it show up for you in the heat of the competitive arena known as hockey. The routine has to be something you do on a daily basis in practice. Game-like practice is critical to your mental game development because it enhances your ability to stick to your routines in pressure situations. Ultimately, the purpose of routines is to provide something physical to assist us with something mental.

Remember, practice makes permanent. You want to drill these routines during your preparation, making them such a permanent part of your performance process that you unconsciously tune into a predetermined mindset for performance excellence. It is also worth noting that you should approach your routine in the same manner you approach the entire performance – with quality effort, attention to detail, and present-moment focus on the process.

Breaking down all elements of your performance into routines will ultimately make it a routine performance and give you the structure that will enable you to develop performance excellence and play one shift at a time. Making performance skills routine ultimately makes the experience of climbing The Mountain of Hockey Excellence feel much simpler and gives you a tremendous boost of confidence.

CHAPTER #6 REVIEW

- ☐ The secrets of success are hidden in the routines of our daily lives.

- ☐ Pre-game and post-game routines are important to get yourself into and out of your performance mentality.

- ☐ In-game routines enhance self-control.

- ☐ Step into your circle of focus during performance.

- ☐ Establish a final thought for performance tasks.

- ☐ Superman used segmentation and separation techniques, and so should you.

- ☐ Move through the hourglass for performance self-transformation.

- ☐ Lace it up and lock it in to be Gladiator ready.

- ☐ During performance, use focal points to mentally check in.

- ☐ Integrate taking a deep breath into your performance routines.

- ☐ Performance routines must be regularly practiced to maximize their potentials.

CHAPTER #7

RECOGNIZE, RELEASE, REFOCUS

> "The athlete should be taught that he will give his best effort whenever he competes, mentally and physically. That he will focus on his performance goals, not the expectations of others, focusing on executing the task of the moment, bringing a relaxed intensity and a relentless spirit to the competition."
>
> **Harvey Dorfman**
> **Sport Psychologist**

Recognizing your physical, emotional and mental state within the context of your competitive environment is critical to staying in control of yourself, thereby giving yourself the best opportunity for success.

The development of a routine in which you recognize where you are at mentally, emotionally and physically and where you have a release to use when you are in a negative place so that you can refocus on the next shift is an essential part of playing hockey one shift at a time.

This chapter will give you the skills to develop your own one-shift-at-a-time mental management system to keep your state of mind active and engaged in the moment as you journey up The Mountain of Hockey Excellence.

RECOGNIZING YOUR SIGNAL LIGHTS

The most challenging aspect of the mental game is learning to recognize when your performance is taking a turn for the worse and then developing a system to make the necessary corrections to return to a place of performance excellence.

The recognition that you are having a performance breakdown is the primary and most crucial step in the process of playing one shift at a time. Recognizing where you are – mentally, emotionally, and physically – is called your Awareness To Win (#ATW). Nobody is perfect. All hockey coaches and players lose control of themselves on occasion, but it is the performer who can correct himself the quickest who tends to perform consistently and, ultimately, has more success.

SIGNAL LIGHTS FOR HOCKEY EXPLAINED

If you are driving a car and you come to a green light, you would naturally GO! If you are driving a car and the light turns yellow, some of us would slow down while others would speed up, depending on where we are in relation to the light. When you come to a red light, however, you must stop or you are going to crash and burn. Now, if you are reading this chuckling to yourself about the time you ran a red light and didn't cause an accident or get caught by the police, then I am with you. However, we must caution against such consistent action – because you might run a red light once and live, but do it routinely and you will crash and burn.

CAIN'S COACHING POINT:

Be aware of your signal lights in hockey. If you run through red lights, you will crash and burn. Play as many shifts as you can in green lights to give yourself the best chance for success.

Performance awareness in hockey is similar to driving a car on the road. When you have green lights (positive, confident, specific, and aggressive thoughts and feelings), you are in control of yourself. In performance, you encounter yellow lights (hopeful, uncertain, vague, and timid thoughts and feelings), which occur when something negative happens to take you out of a green light mentality. If your yellow lights are not recognized and addressed, then you will often find yourself in red lights (negative, dejected, apathetic, and destructive thoughts and feelings). Playing in yellow or red lights is a recipe for beating yourself with a poor performance.

The easiest way for you to think about your signal lights is this:

Green – You are giving yourself the best opportunity for performance excellence.

Yellow – You are starting to lose the mentality conducive to peak performance.

Red – You are totally out of control and it is reflecting in your performance.

The goal of all peak performers is to play the game of hockey with green lights as much as possible, while focusing on the next 200 feet of the journey.

CAUSES OF YELLOW & RED LIGHTS

One thing that makes hockey such a unique and special game is the athleticism and stamina required to play. It is this fast-paced, ever-changing direction that draws so many of us to the sport, because it provides a tremendous excitement like no other game. It truly is the fastest sport on the planet! The fast-paced physical stamina, however, creates fatigue. Any player that ever played hockey has experienced tremendous fatigue. Nothing will remove you from your green light mentality faster than fatigue. It will lead to mental mistakes and thus, during competition, yellow and red lights could result. Some other examples of yellow and red lights are making a costly turnover, an official making a bad call, a coach's criticism, fans getting on your nerves, your opponent talking trash, or any number of other things that can become stuck in your head.

Adversity comes in all forms, physical and mental, and does not have to involve events within your performance environment. The world outside of your performance arena also can affect your performance if you are not in control of yourself. These might include that grudge against your boss, the schoolwork you must accomplish or your latest love interest. Do not let these things distract you from your present-moment focus and peak performance mentality of competing one shift at a time. Focusing on what you are trying to avoid, instead of what you are trying to accomplish, is a recipe for disastrous performance and a signal that you are in a yellow or red light.

In hockey, if your mind is illuminated by the red lights of a negative mentality, you are nearly guaranteed to be on the losing end of your competition.

THREE WAYS TO RECOGNIZE YOUR SIGNAL LIGHTS

There are three major areas in which you can develop your performance awareness and learn to better recognize your signal lights. The three areas in which you can often recognize where you are at mentally, physically, and emotionally are these:

1. Self-talk – What you are saying to yourself

2. Physical feelings – How you are feeling, physically

3. Situations – Circumstances which arise in performance that will trigger particular signal lights

CAIN'S COACHING POINT:

The purpose of routines is to maintain self-control and get into a green light performance mentality as often as possible.

GREEN LIGHTS – THE CAT MENTALITY

Green lights are an easy concept to comprehend. They represent the mentality of peak performance; where you are feeling positive, aggressive, and confident; focused on the present process at hand; and in control of your performance thoughts and actions. Green lights are performance movers and confidence builders. One hockey player I worked with referred to the green light mentality as the CAT mentality – Confident, Aggressive and Tough.

When you are confident, aggressive and tough, you are locked into the moment and moving forward with green lights. Staying in the green light zone, you give yourself the best opportunity to have an excellent performance on this shift.

In order to recognize when you are not in a green light state of mind, you must first recognize what signs indicate that you are in the green. The next three sections will help you use the three major areas of signal light recognition to identify your green light mentality.

GREEN LIGHTS – SELF-TALK

When you have green lights, what are you saying to yourself? Some examples could be:

1. I am unbeatable!

2. I own this rink; this is my house.

3. I make a difference every shift.

4. I am a winner. We are winners.

Green light thoughts are much like your confidence conditioning statements, but they are shorter and very specific to your athletic performance. They are usually aggressive, external, specific and confident thoughts.

CAIN'S COACHING POINT:

Write down your green light thoughts – what do you say to yourself when you are playing at your best?

_____

_____

GREEN LIGHTS – PHYSICAL FEELINGS

When you have green lights, how do you feel physically?

Most hockey players report:

1. I feel light on my feet.

2. My muscles are relaxed and I have good energy.

3. I feel strong and I have big body language.

CAIN'S COACHING POINT:

Write down your green light feelings – how do you feel about yourself when you are playing at your best?

_____

_____

_____

GREEN LIGHTS – SITUATIONS

What situations or actions in competition, practice, the weight room or academic settings put you into green lights?

Most hockey players report:

1. When I have a great warm-up

2. When I have had a good night's sleep

3. When I practiced my presentation over and over, so I knew the content forward and backward

4. When I stick with my routine

CAIN'S COACHING POINT:

Write down the situations in performance that will place you into your green light – the situations where you know you will play at your best.

_____

_____

RED & YELLOW LIGHTS

Hockey players I have worked with in the past have occasionally become caught up in trying to identify whether they were in a red light or yellow light. As an athlete, I want you not to get hung up on that distinction because it is counterproductive to peak performance. This distinction is more relevant for coaches because they must discern which measure will help you get back into your green light mentality – coaching you on taking a deep breath, calling a time-out or making a substitution.

As an athlete, the distinction does not matter as much. Red lights are negative thoughts, confidence cutters, and performance stoppers – and yellow leads you there. Green is where you want to be. All you need to identify is whether or not you are giving yourself the green light. If you are not in the green, then recognize, release and refocus on the performance at hand. The next three sections will help you use the three major areas of signal light recognition to identify whether you are in red/yellow lights.

RED/YELLOW LIGHTS – SELF-TALK

When you have red/yellow lights, what are you saying to yourself?

Most hockey players report:

1. I cannot believe the official made that call.

2. Why is coach saying that?

3. Why can't I score?

4. Why do I play this stupid game?

5. I suck.

CAIN'S COACHING POINT:

Write down your red/yellow light thoughts – what do you say to yourself when you are struggling on the ice?

_____

_____

RED/YELLOW LIGHTS – PHYSICAL FEELINGS

When you have red/yellow lights, how do you feel physically?

Most hockey players report:

1. I do not feel good; I feel tired and slow; I have no kick.

2. I feel like I cannot catch my breath.

3. The atmosphere is intimidating.

4. The puck has been bouncing all night.

5. I feel like the game's speeding up on me.

CAIN'S COACHING POINT:

Write down your red/yellow light feelings – what do you feel physically when you are struggling on the rink?

_____

_____

RED/YELLOW LIGHTS – SITUATIONS

What situations or actions in competition, practice, the weight room or academic settings put you into red/yellow lights?

Most hockey players report:

1. When I make a mental error

2. When an official makes a bad call

3. When my line mate makes a bad play

4. When I know I could have prepared better

CAIN'S COACHING POINT:

Write down what situations in performance will put you into a red/yellow light and what happens when you are playing at your worst. What removes you from your green light mentality?

_____

_____

SIGNAL LIGHTS = PERFORMANCE CHANGE

Once you have identified your self-talk, your physical feelings and the situations that put you into your green and red/yellow lights, you immediately give yourself a better chance to recognize your signal lights in performance. If you have green lights, refocus on the next play. If you have red/yellow lights, you must release before you refocus.

Remember the three steps to performance change:

1. Develop awareness of what needs to change.

2. Develop a strategy for change to happen.

3. Put that strategy into action.

Most athletes do not know how to make necessary performance adjustments because they have not developed performance awareness. Performance change is all about understanding your internal signal lights. **Mentally, what you are aware of you can control; what you are unaware of is going to control you**. This is why understanding and practicing the signal lights concept gives you the best opportunity to effectively exercise the three steps of performance change.

INVERTED U OF SIGNAL LIGHTS

Peak Performance 101 is about understanding the Inverted U.

On the North-South axis we have performance, and on the East-West axis there is intensity or focus.

How excited are you?

When you are not intense or focused enough, performance is low. Conversely, when you are overly intense or are too focused and trying too hard, performance is still low. This is why it is important for peak performers to maintain a consistent mental state of excellence to compete with optimal energy and perform at their best on a consistent shift-to-shift basis. Your in-game routines and, most importantly, your deep breath allow you to manage your mental, emotional and physical self to stay in the moment and at your peak of optimal energy on the Inverted U of Performance.

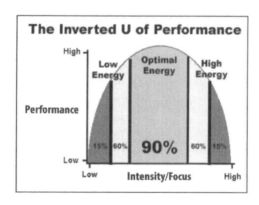

This mental state of performance excellence is maintained through the adoption of performance routines that create a mental management. A mental management routine takes you from falling just anywhere on the inverted U and gives you a much better chance of consistently falling in the center, which is your optimal energy and arousal area for a peak performance. This routine-based mental maintenance system gives you the best chance of performing at the peak of the Inverted U.

PERFORMANCE ROUTINES

Performance routines are the life jacket of peak performance. When the pressure is on, as it usually is in hockey, you turn to your routines so that you can stay in the present moment and increase your chances of achieving performance excellence on the next shift. The importance of routines to performance is a simple formula: Routines lead to consistency, consistency leads to confidence, and confidence leads to success.

CAIN'S COACHING POINT:

To be consistent over time, you must be able to describe what you do as a process/routine.

The best hockey programs I have worked with as a mental conditioning coach have specific systems and structured performance routines that help players perform consistently over the course of the game and the season. These programs often stress the importance of having a focal point to turn to during pressure performances. When you get distracted or you have red/yellow light thoughts and start beating yourself up, your focal point is your box of positive thoughts – they represent your checkpoint to help you slow down and get back into your green lights.

RELEASE

Once you have learned to recognize your signal lights, the next step in the process is developing a release routine to help you rid yourself of the negative emotion that will slow you down.

The purpose of your release/physical routine is to help you get back in control of yourself and back into your green lights.

This release routine facilitates your transition back to a green light mentality. When you are in red/yellow lights, you must develop some sort of physical routine to help you mentally release the negative frustration. This physical action should be an expressive release to get control of your mental state and return you to the pursuit of performance excellence on the next shift.

CAIN'S COACHING POINT:

Examples of common releases are to take your gloves off, take a deep breath, or unlace and lace up your skates again, take a sip of water and spit it out, read a focus word on your wristband. What are physical releases you can use to help you get from red/yellow lights and back to green?

_____

_____

RELEASE YOUR MENTAL BRICKS

A hockey coach told me how he dealt with getting players to release their mental bricks. He purchased a fake "rubber" brick from a prop store and uses it when needed to make the point about releasing your mental bricks. If a player is exhibiting a "mental brick" during practice, then he simply hands over the "rubber" brick and asks that person to continue practicing while holding onto the "rubber" brick. Quickly the player complains that he/she can't practice holding onto the brick. The coach then pulls that player aside and explains that this is exactly correct and that performance will be the same until he or she releases the mental brick. The mental brick is prohibiting the player from performing at the highest level. The reality is that at one point or another, we all make errors and mistakes or fall prey to unrealistic expectations. There is a common tendency to continue to carry these mistakes and poor performances with us, resulting in a buildup of negative mental energy. Instead of beating yourself up over a poor performance, you must learn to release these "mental bricks" that weigh on your mind.

If, every time you make a mistake, you were to grab a physical brick and carry that brick with you, it would weigh you down both physically and mentally. This would invariably inhibit you from performing to the best of your ability.

Now, visualize a mistake you are bitter about as a mental brick. When you carry this mistake with you, this mental brick, it takes the same toll as carrying a physical brick. The difference is that you cannot see it because it is a weight within your mind.

In your quest for excellence, you must train yourself to release the mental bricks that threaten to weigh you down. Releasing your mental bricks relies on a process of reflection and realization followed by the release. After a mistake or a poor performance, you must thoughtfully reflect on the experience and consider how you can improve. Once you have realized what improvements can be made in your performance, you can then release the error from your consciousness and move on to the next shift. The release process should happen on the bench in between shifts or at a whistle and happen as quickly as possible. ***Releasing a negative shift or play and getting to the next shift is a skill that must be developed through repetition.***

EXAMPLES OF IN-GAME RELEASES

In-game releases should be directed at a consistent focal point. Your focal point could be an object somewhere in the rink or on a part of your uniform. Whatever that focal point may be, when you look at it, you should take a good deep breath, push out your chest, get big and put all of that red/yellow light, negative energy and self-doubt into that focal point and let it go.

As you transfer that energy, remind yourself to get back to the next play and what's important now (#WIN) and return to your green light thoughts and green light/refocus routine.

You could wipe the snow off your skates and throw it on the ground, same with the snow from your stick blade, take a deep breath, snap a rubber band or wristband and release. This physical action allows you to make a mental connection to the next shift. Players can take off their gloves while sitting on the bench, find the focal point in the rink, take two deep breaths, etc. In the process, they get rid of the last shift and can then refocus on the most important shift of the game... the next one!

Some coaches want their players to all have the same release, such as wiping snow off their blade and taking a deep breath, so that they only have to watch for one release from everyone. Whether you have each player come up with his/her own, do it by position or have the entire team use the same release, that is up to you as the coach. Each release should have something physical that they do plus a deep breath.

Here are some more examples of release routines:

You can shake your hands to shake off the red/yellow light thoughts.

You can make a fist, and as you release your fingers, release the past play.

There are hundreds of different releases you can use. The important part of the release is to be sure that you have something physical that you do, and that you are taking a deep breath and have a focal point as a part of your release.

FLUSH IT

A fun way to think about releasing mental bricks is by conjuring the image of a toilet. When you have a mental brick that is in danger of putting you in red lights, you want to take this mental brick and "flush it." Once you are relieved of that mental brick, you are ready to return to the present moment in your performance.

University of Vermont Men's Hockey head coach Kevin Sneddon took this concept and integrated it into part of his team's post-performance routine. He keeps a miniature foam toilet in the team dressing room, and after a frustrating period or a hard-fought game, he and his players will flush the mental bricks from their performance.

"I ask each of my players to flush the game down the toilet and move on," says Coach Sneddon. "The visual works quite well."

It is inevitable, as you climb The Mountain of Hockey Excellence, that you will face forms of adversity that weigh on your mind. Do not carry these mental bricks with you on your journey. Stop routinely at your mental toilet to relieve yourself of their weight. Perform your release routine to flush away the negativity built within those mental bricks. Your mind will feel lighter and clearer, and you will be more mentally agile when you get back to your climb of playing the next play.

REFOCUS ON THE NEXT SHIFT

Once you recognize your signal lights and release your red/yellow lights with your release routine, it becomes critical that you refocus back into the present moment and on the next shift.

Refocusing returns your mind to the next shift and pushes you towards performance excellence. One of the best ways you can refocus is to talk out loud with your teammates during competition. *When you talk out loud, you are external and present*. When you are quiet, you can easily get lost in your own head, thinking about the past or the future. Refocus back to the present moment – you will give yourself the best chance to perform at your best by talking out loud and being an energy giver.

SO WHAT, NEXT SHIFT! MENTALITY

Let me ask you this. Are you that bad that every call and every bounce has to go your way to win? If the answer is no, why do you get so angry when an official makes a bad call or a play doesn't go your way?

Keep in mind that great plays are as much of a pitfall for players and coaches in terms of refocusing. It is critical that you flush away the excitement and thrill of the great move you just made – or that call from the official – and get in the moment as soon as possible.

Refocusing, just like all mental conditioning, requires that your mind and body work together. If your body is trying to play the game in the moment and your mind is still analyzing a previous play/shift or thinking about the possibility of a play in the future, your mind and body are working against each other and you lose.

You want to live in the big picture and compete in the moment. When things aren't going your way, you have got to embrace adversity. Say "So What, Next Shift!" Let go of the past, and get back to competing in the present moment and executing on the next play.

"So What, Next Shift!" is a verbal key that you can use to help refocus you and your teammates back into the present moment. This key helps you bridge from the past by saying "So What" and returns you where you want to be in the present by saying "Next Shift."

You cannot just say "So What, Next Shift!" with your mouth; you have to say it with your body as well. By using your physical release routine to return to the present, regardless of how you feel about the past play/shift, saying "So What, Next Shift!" refocuses your mind. You can then actively engage in the most important part of your performance – the next 200 feet.

In life and hockey, negative things happen. Adversity is going to strike and there is nothing you can do to stop it. And why would you want to stop adversity? Adversity is a positive. Adversity is what causes you to grow. Adversity and success are neighbors on the highway to excellence; you can't get one without the other.

Some tragedies are simply outside of your control. What you cannot do is allow yourself to get caught up in a moment that has already passed. You must constantly move on to the next shift. This "So What, Next Shift!" mentality is the hallmark of a peak performer on the ice.

REFOCUS SIGN

When I go to work with top hockey teams, I like to hang a sign on their bench that says "REFOCUS." I teach the players that when they recognize their minds starting to wander, they only have to look at the sign and refocus. Using the sign as a focal point gets them back into the next shift. This is another very simple yet highly effective tool to help you get back into the present moment.

THE RECOGNIZE – RELEASE – REFOCUS CYCLE

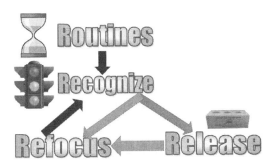

The process of recognize-release-refocus is an important one to master in your pursuit of performance excellence in hockey. This process is founded on an internal awareness of your signal lights, especially the ability to recognize when you are out of your green light mentality. Upon recognizing your yellow or red light state of mind, you must make a present-moment performance change by performing your release routine in order to refocus for the next shift.

This process is conceptually simple and highly effective, yet it is amazing how many athletes neglect this cycle to maximize their performance potential.

This is one of the mental conditioning systems that separate the good from the great performers. If you want to perform at a consistently high level of excellence, you must learn how to recognize your signal lights, release frustration from past plays, and refocus on the present moment in competition.

CAIN'S COACHING POINT:

When you have adversity and bad calls that go against you, use the verbal for release & refocus, which is "So What, Next Shift!"

A REALISTIC LOOK AT "THE ZONE"

I do not think you will ever be in green lights for an entire game. If you find yourself in "The Zone," with that relaxed intensity and your green lights on steady, then enjoy the ride, baby, 'cause it does not happen often!

It is an experience you may have once – maybe never. Over the careers of the greatest performers on the planet, this kind of "zone" may happen only a handful of times.

Peak performance is not about being in "The Zone" all the time and having everything in the game go your way. Adversity is built into the fabric of hockey, making every competition unique and full of new variables and situations for players to overcome.

Peak performance is about playing your best when you need it the most, each and every play. It is about compensating and adjusting your performance to the present-moment conditions of performance. It is about handling and managing pressure better than the opposition. It is about rolling with the punches until you get the job done. The better your routines and the more systematic your approach, the better your chance to stay in the green lights and perform on the level of excellence one shift at a time.

Great athletes embrace adversity. They welcome it and they starve for it, because they know their ability to overcome adversity is what makes them great. The more adverse the conditions that day for both teams, the better they play because they know they are better equipped than the opponent is to handle adversity.

KNOW YOUR 4R CYCLE

You want to work on your release and refocus routines every day just like you do your skating or team's systems in hockey. It may be for only two minutes. As part of your in-competition *Routine*, you want to work on your ability to *Recognize* your physical and mental state, *Release,* and *Refocus* on the next shift every day in practice.

If you know what your red/yellow lights are and you fail to make a performance change by implementing release and refocus routines to return to your green light mentality, then you are not maximizing your performance potential. You are no better off than your competitor who has not invested the time to read this book and has not cultivated a deeper understanding of the mental game of hockey.

Knowing what to do but not doing what you know means you are no better off than the person who has no idea what to do. ***Be a "Do-er," not a "Know-er."***

CHAPTER #7 REVIEW

- [ ] The ability to recognize your physical, emotional and mental state within the context of your competitive environment is absolutely necessary.

- [ ] Green signal lights – you are giving yourself the best opportunity for performance excellence.

- [ ] Yellow signal lights – you are starting to lose the mentality conducive to peak performance.

- [ ] Red signal lights – you are totally out of control and it is reflecting in your performance.

- [ ] Mastery of performance awareness is developed by understanding your self-talk, physical feelings, and how you deal with common situations during performance.

- [ ] A routine-based mental maintenance system keeps you at the peak of the Inverted U of Performance.

- [ ] To be consistent over time, you must be able to describe your routines as a process.

- [ ] The purpose of your release/physical routine is to help you get back in control of yourself and back into your green lights.

- [ ] Release your mental bricks.

- [ ] All releases should be directed at a consistent focal point.

- [ ] Be sure to take a deep breath during your release.

- [ ] When you have a mental brick, relieve your mind and "Flush It."

- [ ] Refocus on WIN (What's Important Now).

- [ ] Develop a "So What, Next Shift!" mentality to refocus when adversity strikes.

- Use a refocus sign as a focal point.

- Peak performance is not about being in "The Zone." It is about making the necessary adjustments to perform consistently at a level of excellence and to be able to compensate and adjust.

CHAPTER #8

RESPONSE-ABILITY

"Mental toughness is many things and rather difficult to explain. Its qualities are sacrifice and self-denial. Also, most importantly, it is combined with a perfectly disciplined will that refuses to give in. It's a state of mind – you could call it character in action."

Vince Lombardi
NFL coach, Hall of Famer

The most powerful ten-word sentence in the English language consists of only seven short two-letter words. That sentence is: *If it is to be, it is up to me.* This encapsulates response-ability.

Response-ability is taking ownership of your past, commanding your present and taking charge of your future. It is being accountable for your perspective and controlling how you choose to respond to adversity. Too many people are negatively affected by outside influences they cannot control. They respond by becoming a victim of outside factors, rather than responding to adversity by holding themselves responsible for their actions. *Choosing your response in any situation is the greatest of all personal powers we possess as human beings.*

In this chapter, the importance of response-ability will be made clear. You will learn how response-ability makes a difference in performance and how to begin disciplining your mind to respond to events in order to produce productive outcomes.

MAN FREEZES TO DEATH – LACK OF RESPONSE-ABILITY

In the February 1978 issue of *Success Unlimited*, psychologist Dr. Dudley Calvert tells the story of a railway employee in Russia who accidentally locked himself in a refrigerator car. Inside the car, he could not unlock the door nor could he attract the attention of those outside. Unable to escape, he resigned himself to his fate. As he felt his body becoming numb, he documented his story and his approaching death in sentences scribbled on the wall of the car.

"I am becoming colder now," he wrote. "Still colder, now I can hardly write..." and, finally, "these may be my last words." And they were.

When the car was opened upon arrival at its destination, other railway employees found him dead. Yet, the temperature of the car was 56 DEGREES! The freezing apparatus had been out of order in the car and was inaccurately stuck on 28 degrees. There was no physical reason for his death. There was plenty of air – he hadn't suffocated. What happened was he gave away his personal power and defeated himself by not responding appropriately to the challenges in front of him. He let the power of his mind negatively affect his reality. ***Remember, perspective is reality and you are response-able for choosing any attitude and any perspective you want in any given situation.*** His own lack of response-ability led to his demise, a victim of his own delusion.

MAN OVERCOMES HELL ON EARTH – RESPONSE-ABILITY

In *Man's Search for Meaning*, Viktor Frankl talks about his unfathomable experience and survival of the Nazi concentration camps in World War II. Frankl, a psychologist, knew he was response-able for his mental state and only chance at survival in his hell-on-earth conditions. He chose to search for something of value and meaning every day of his struggle.

Living in the concentration camp, Frankl discovered the Nazis could take away his family, his freedom, his food and health, but they could not take away the last of the human freedoms: one's ability to choose his/her own attitude. Frankl realized that his ability to determine how he responded to his environment was psychological and that his human spirit was still free. With this in mind, he found daily existential meaning and purpose in aiding other prisoners by sharing the little food he did have and offering comforting words.

Unlike our man in the boxcar who went down the path of negativity, Frankl chose a path of positive empowerment. Both men had response-ability. If Frankl could find meaning in and survive the horrific experience of the concentration camps, and a man can freeze to death in a non-freezing boxcar, imagine what your response-ability can do for you. Imagine what you can endure.

Have you seen the movie *The Lone Survivor*? The story of Operation Red Wing. That movie shows what the human will can endure. Can you survive the perceived challenges of your everyday life and maintain a positive attitude? Absolutely! To be a peak performer, a sense of response-ability is a must.

EVENT + RESPONSE = OUTCOME

There is a simple math equation that I want you to learn and, more importantly, implement on a daily basis.

E [Event] + R [Response] = O [Outcome]

In life, it is not what happens to you; it is how you handle what happens to you. It is your ability to respond (response-ability) that is going to determine your outcome when adversity is thrown your way.

As a human being, YOU have the ability to respond to an event in the manner you deem appropriate. The response is your choice. Humans have the unique ability to socialize their innate responses to events with the three steps of performance improvement: (1) awareness, (2) strategy and (3) implementation of the strategy. We have previously discussed this process, and it provides an essential foundation for full comprehension of E + R = O.

We often do not have much control over the Events in our lives, but we do control our Responses. This is an empowering notion, because once you realize that you control half the equation, you recognize that you control half the Outcome. If a negative event occurs and you keep a positive present-moment focus with a big-picture mentality and a "Compared to what?" perspective as your response, then you will significantly influence the outcome in your favor.

This is the process of mental conditioning that you prepare for thoroughly establishing mental routines. The practice of mental conditioning will teach you how to be responsible by accepting the Events, formulating Responses and, therefore, perceiving the Outcomes.

We are all capable of using this process to our benefit in life because we all have the ability to control our responses. We all have personal power.

THE HUMAN PAUSE

As was briefly mentioned, humans have the unique ability to become internally aware of their responses to external stimuli. The famous psychological study known as Pavlov's Dog Experiments represents groundbreaking research investigating conditioned and unconditioned responses to unconditioned and conditioned stimuli. Without going into all the details of classical (Pavlovian) conditioning, the takeaway relevant to mental conditioning is when there is a stimulus, there is a response.

Humans are no different, except for our ability to become aware of our responses. This recognition of how we respond is vital to mental conditioning, because we can train ourselves to pause in between the stimulus and our response, again giving us personal power to choose our response. Once we are aware of our innate responses to certain stimuli, we have the power to control and change them. Most people are unaware of this unique human ability, and these are the people we say have poor self-control skills. What they have is a non-trained pause to adversity and negative events.

Start becoming aware of how you respond to certain stimuli. To gain awareness and challenge yourself to catch that pause in between the event and your reaction, reflect on how you react to particular events. Those trained in discipline and response-ability face adverse stimuli with poise. They control their pause by taking a deep breath and responding in a manner conducive to the attainment of excellence. Developing control over that pause is what separates those who stay in control under pressure and those who crack.

Remember it this way: When the dog of adversity threatens with his dangerous jaws, control yourself with your human pause... and deep breath.

EMOTION CLOUDS REALITY

In the heat of competition, it is easy for your mind to become clouded by adversity. When officials make poor calls, the opposition seems to be catching lucky breaks, or you are just not performing to your full potential on that day, it is easy to let your emotions get the best of your performance. As a hockey player in pursuit of excellence, do not let your emotions cloud the reality of performance.

When you take emotion out of the picture, you tend to respond much more clearly. What does emotion do? Emotion clouds reality. In my work in the mental game of hockey, I see frustrated people fire off at officials, coaches, players and athletic directors. These people often approach minor and trivial situations as if they were life or death, not hockey. Most times after the outburst, there's regret that emotions overpowered sensible response-ability.

It is important to use the mental conditioning skills we've discussed in this manual to maintain response-ability. This comes back to self-control – recognizing what is within your control and emotionally letting go of everything else. Rely on the "3P's" of peak performance (present, process, positive) as the conscience that reminds you of your ability to respond with excellence rather than emotion. Act out of routine and conditioned/trained response, not emotion.

RAVIZZA'S RULES OF CONTROL

The greatest coach I have ever had was my mentor at Cal State Fullerton, and he is an icon in the field of sport psychology. Dr. Ken Ravizza introduced me to his three rules of mental conditioning that I believe truly reflect the significance of response-ability as it relates to hockey.

I believe a peak performer on the ice must understand those rules of response-ability to give himself/herself the personal power to reach the summit of The Mountain of Hockey Excellence:

1. Before you can control your performance, you must be in control of yourself.

2. You have very little control of what goes on around you, but you have total control over how you choose to respond to it.

3. What you are aware of you can control; what you are unaware of will control you.

Staying in control of yourself and recognizing what you can and cannot control will allow you to mentally stay in a calm, centered and grounded place. Staying in control of yourself in the face of adversity is a skill set that must be repetitively practiced for its proper development and will allow you to perform in pressure situations.

Understanding what you can and cannot control, and choosing to focus on what you can control while letting go of what you cannot, gives you the personal power to focus your time, energy and attention to achieve excellence.

The first step to self-control is having an awareness of what is going on around you and, more importantly, what is going on inside of you. Ultimately, the development of self-awareness will place the power of response-ability in your head and in your hands.

CAIN'S COACHING POINT:

Early on in the manual, you learned the importance of forcing yourself to act differently than how you feel, shouldering that personal response-ability, and choosing to act appropriately regardless of the situation. How have you been doing at acting differently than how you feel? Where in your life can you act differently than how you feel, choosing your response, and giving yourself a better chance for success?

_____

_____

_____

PRAYER, PRIMAL, PERFECT?

In his book *Heads-Up Baseball*, Dr. Ken Ravizza points out that when athletes get emotionally out of control, it usually manifests through their performance in three general ways. They become a Prayer, Primal, or Perfect performer, all of which lead to a decreased level of performance.

PRAYER: When you become the prayer player, you look to some higher power to help you perform. You resign to faith in fate and simply hope for the stars to align and present you with the desired result.

PRIMAL: When you become a primal player, you resort back to the days of the caveman. You begin to perform in a desperate and erratic manner that often leaves you out of control and emotionally frustrated, and the desired result remains elusive.

PERFECT: When you become the perfect player, you attempt to make everything perfect. You strive for performance perfection and little mistakes prevent you from appreciating the beautiful imperfections of the game. As we have discussed, performance oriented around perfection is a sure path to failure because nothing is perfect. Remember, performance is not about perfection; it is about progress.

As a performer, you DO NOT want to fall under any of these three categories of Prayer, Primal or Perfect.

The defining question at the highest levels of competition is not who has the most physical talent, because physical talent is, for the most part, similar at the highest levels of performance. Were the 8th seeded Los Angeles Kings the most talented and best team in the NHL when they won the cup in 2012? Does the winner of the Presidents' Trophy always win the Stanley Cup? Instead, the question pertains to who is able to bring his/her mental talents to the table on a consistent basis and who has the ability to respond appropriately under the pressures of adversity.

As a hockey player, you want to move away from Prayer, Primal and Perfect and into PREPARED and PRESENT. Mental preparation will assist you in the development of appropriate response-ability, giving yourself the best opportunity for performance excellence, one play at a time.

TRAIN YOUR RESPONSE-ABILITY

Coach Bear Bryant understood that football was the premiere vehicle for training response-ability. When he arrived at Alabama in 1958, he said: "We are going to do two things. We are going to learn to play football, and we are going to get up and go to class like our mamas and papas expect us to. And we are going to win. Ten years from now, you are going to be married with a family. Your wife might be sick, your kids might be sick, you might be sick, but you will get your butt up and go to work. That's what I'm going to do for you. I'm going to teach you how to do things you don't feel like doing." This analogy is an awesome example of *"Fake it until you Make it."* This is how you have more good bad days because you do it right even when you don't feel like doing it.

Peak performance is contingent on personal response-ability in daily excellence. Excellence is largely about being accountable for your perspective and controlling your response to the adverse events that will inevitably occur during performance. Use the equation E + R = O as a reminder that you control half of the equation and the outcome is a result of your perspective. When you train your response-ability, you place the power in your head.

All peak performers learn to take ownership of their past, command the present, and take charge of their future. Once you instill these values within your performance, you will gain the self-control necessary for performance excellence. Do not become a victim to events. Become a champion by developing the ability to respond appropriately to adversity. We all have the ability to respond appropriately, and the material throughout this book gives you the resources to do just that.

The Mountain of Hockey Excellence and the game of hockey call out to many performers, but the ones who reach the peak are those who have the response-ability to master the journey and overcome the adversity. The Mountain of Hockey Excellence will put obstacles in your path and humble you at times, just like hockey and just like life.

CHAPTER #8 REVIEW

☐ If it is to be, it is up to me.

☐ Response-ability is taking ownership of your past, commanding your present and taking charge of your future.

☐ Event + Response = Outcome.

☐ When the dog of adversity threatens with his dangerous jaws, control yourself with your human pause.

☐ Emotion clouds reality; learn to control it.

☐ Develop self-control by learning the three rules of response-ability.

☐ Prayer, Primal and Perfect are all undesirable states of performance mentality.

CHAPTER #9

RELAX & RECOVER
MENTAL IMAGERY

> "In warfare, there are no constant conditions. He who can modify his tactics in relation to his opponent will succeed and win."
>
> **Sun Tzu**
> **The Art of War**

Most hockey coaches and players that I work with have a hard time relaxing. This is often due to the competitive and combative nature and the aggressive mentality it takes to play this physically demanding game at a high level. As a peak performer, you spend a lot of time acting differently than how you feel and forcing yourself to keep on grinding and working to take your performance to the next level.

Another reason why many hockey coaches and players have a hard time relaxing is that a large part of their lives is spent making themselves do the things they may not feel like doing but that are instrumental to peak performance on the ice. This shows their necessary dedication and resolve to being the best; however, quality time devoted to relaxation and recovery is also necessary to maximize performance potential. **The harder you work, the more important recovery is to regeneration so that you can continue to work and train at a high level.**

The ability to relax is essential to peak performers, and it is fundamental to developing peace of mind both during and away from the ice. When it comes to your ability to relax, you cannot make yourself relax; you must *let* yourself relax, and this is where hockey players and coaches often find the challenge.

This performance state seems diametrically opposed to the intense focus demanded for performance excellence on the ice and is therefore difficult for most to achieve. When you are in a relaxed state, however, your heart rate is lower, your breathing becomes deeper, and this kick-starts the recovery/repair process for the body and brain. The more relaxed you are, the quicker you recover from the demands you place on yourself and the quicker you can get back to performance and preparation at the highest level.

CAIN'S COACHING POINT:

Relaxation is a skill that must be practiced and is a skill that can be developed with proper training, just like the fundamental physical skills of playing hockey.

THE ABILITY TO RELAX IS INSIDE YOU

Everything you need to relax is already inside you. The world's most powerful tranquilizers already reside within your body. You have the ability to use these tranquilizers to put yourself to sleep at night, and you can train yourself to tap into one of the most powerful resources of your body and mind throughout the day when you experience stress, pressure and anxiety.

Hockey players have reported to me that if they could relax, it would help their performance. Knowing they need to relax is not the problem; the problem is that they often do not know how, because they have never been taught the simple strategy for relaxation.

Let's face it. When a coach or teammate says to you, "Hey, Brian, just relax!" (which I heard my entire career as an athlete) it does nothing to help your performance. In reality, it often makes you more tense, because now you know that your teammate or coach has picked up on the fact that you are stressed out and full of anxiety. As a player or coach, instead of telling someone to relax, ask him to take a good deep breath. Taking a deep breath is the single most valuable and effective exercise the athlete must learn to use to enter a more relaxed and present state.

THE CALMING OF CAIN

When I was a college baseball player at The University of Vermont, and a high school quarterback, the part of my game that held me back the most was my inability to relax and keep my mind productively focused in the present moment, one pitch/play at a time. My mind would get moving so fast that I could not keep it on the one thought that mattered, the execution of that particular pitch/play. My mind would be thinking about how this was my opportunity to make up for my previous mistakes; to finally show my coaches, teammates, and myself that I was good; that I was worthy of the scholarship or the playing time I had been given; and that, if I could perform at the level of my expectations, I could be one of the best.

As you can tell, the gears would begin to move faster and faster until I could hardly breathe; and before I knew it, I was ready to come out of the game before it even started.

My senior year of college I took a stress management class with the University of Vermont gymnastics coach Gary Bruning. Luckily for me, it was more of an applied stress management class than a theory-based class. He taught the class *how* to mentally and physically relax instead of teaching textbook theories of stress management and all the physiological effects of stress that I had experienced. I was very aware of the fact I did not know how to relax, so I embraced the opportunity for self-improvement as Coach Bruning taught us all how to relax.

He had us lie down on the floor and talked us through a deep-breathing exercise. I put my hand on my stomach and focused intently on breathing in through my nostrils and out through my mouth, while feeling my stomach rise with the inhalation and lower with the exhalation of each breath. After about 5 minutes of feeling weird just lying there and feeling like I should be doing something else, with my mind racing 100MPH, I finally experienced my mind slowing down and my body and mind relaxing.

I was 22 years old, a senior in college, and I can still vividly remember experiencing the ability to relax for the first time in my life. It was a revolutionary mind-body experience, and utterly unfamiliar to me. I could slow my mind down and focus into the present through my newfound ability to relax. I could now also speed up my recovery process simply by focusing on my breathing. To this day, I am grateful that I enrolled in that course and for Coach Bruening's applied method of teaching.

MAXIMIZING OXYGEN IN THE OCTAGON

As a mental conditioning coach, nowhere have I seen relaxation and deep breathing serve a more vital function for performance excellence than in the Ultimate Fighting Championship. The world's most combative, most competitive sport of mixed martial arts is a ballet of violence by nature. Some people may find it too brutal for their liking, but this cannot discredit the impressive mentality it takes to step inside of the Octagon and go to battle. As athletes and coaches, we can learn a lot from what happens mentally inside the Octagon that can assist peak performance in hockey. In my work with college and high school hockey programs, I teach a lot of the very same mental skills that I train the best MMA fighters on the planet to have in their mental game arsenal.

In mixed martial arts, it is often the fighter who can relax first and move the fight into his specialty who wins. While the fighters work on bringing the fight to them, some of the greatest coaches in the game can be heard reinforcing the importance of breathing to help their fighter athletes relax. As a coach, the verbal cue for an athlete to take a breath is a reminder of what the athlete must do to calm down and perform at a more relaxed state. The more an athlete practices his breathing exercises to relax and quiet his mind outside of the Octagon, the more the brain and body know how to respond when he takes the deep breath inside the Octagon. As with everything in peak performance, you must learn to be in control of yourself physically and mentally before you can control your performance, and the most crucial practice to gain self-control is deep breathing.

I see getting an MMA fighter to take a deep breath in his corner between rounds the same as a hockey player taking a deep breath on the ice and a coach getting the team to take good deep breaths at the start of a time-out or between shifts.

RELAXED INTENSITY – CONTROLLED RAGE

The best hockey players perform with a relaxed intensity. These players become so immersed in their present-moment focus of execution on that one shift that they are simultaneously calm and poised, yet fully engaged and energized. Their competitive concentration appears unbreakable. Nothing can distract them; no adversity fazes them. They are "locked in" and it is as if they are playing on another level. Well, they ARE on another level; this is performance excellence!

CAIN'S COACHING POINT:

This peak performance state of excellence is different than "The Zone." Personally, I believe "The Zone" to be a place of quiet mind and quiet body where you are performing at your best.

I think "The Zone" is a place that we waste too much time talking about and trying to get to. I do not believe you can recreate "The Zone," but I do believe that you can get much closer to the state of peak performance through mental conditioning of distraction control, battling and dealing with adversity, acting differently than you feel, and competing all out, every shift. I invest my time in coaching how to mentally persevere and have good bad days; I do not focus on getting into "The Zone." Remember, you cannot always control how you feel, but you can choose how you act. Think of confidence as an ACTION more than a feeling.

RELAX FOR RESULTS

Many coaches will ask me to teach them the secret of performance when the pressure to produce results is at its highest. They want me to teach their team how to produce when it is late in the 3rd period and the game is on the line. What they fail to understand, however, is that there is no secret key to unlock performance when you need it the most. The best way a player or team can respond to the situation is to relax and trust in their mental and physical conditioning. This gives them the best chance to execute on the next shift – and executing on the next shift is ALL THAT MATTERS!

So when coaches ask me this question, they are usually surprised when I lead the team away from their performance arena to a quiet and controlled environment and instruct them in methods of breathing and relaxation. The hockey player must be able to relax in a quiet and controlled environment before ever being able to relax in the face of adversity on the ice. The deep breath and ability to relax is the most powerful tool in the peak performance toolbox and is critical to unlocking your potential so that you can become "locked in" during performance.

RELAXATION IS A SKILL ANYONE CAN DEVELOP

As with all mental conditioning techniques, relaxation is a skill that can be learned and developed through training. Relaxation is a skill that requires mastering all the material previously covered in this book. The ability to relax is founded upon a present-moment focus on the process of what you can control, along with a perspective of positivity that has been practiced over and over so that it has become routine.

I want you to think of the ability to relax as a skill just like the physical skills you use in hockey. If you can skate, shoot or stickhandle, your ability to execute that skill is because you have trained yourself to perform it. You have practiced and you have conditioned that skill, investing time and effort into improving it. I want you to do the same for the mental conditioning skill of relaxation.

THE 5-4-3-2-1 RELAXATION/FOCUS EXERCISE

I want to walk you through a relaxation and focus exercise called the 5-4-3-2-1 exercise. By understanding how to breathe properly and practicing the process of a 5-4-3-2-1 relaxation technique until it becomes a routine relaxation procedure, you give yourself the best opportunity to relax under pressure and perform at your best.

CAIN'S COACHING POINT:

I have created a 5-4-3-2-1 relaxation training audio that you can download for free by subscribing to my podcast at www.briancain.com/hockey. There are other great training tools available for you on my podcast as well.

TWO TYPES OF BREATHING

There are two types of breathing: diaphragmatic breathing and shoulder breathing. Diaphragmatic breathing is deep breathing, using your diaphragm and abdominal muscles. To identify this type of breathing, place your hand upon your stomach and feel your abdominal muscles expand as you inhale and contract as you exhale. During this deep breathing, air entirely fills your lungs and maximizes oxygen intake. Shoulder breathing, on the other hand, only reaches the top of your lungs. Often referred to as shallow breathing, shoulder breathing is often the result of a performer's inability to relax, resulting in tight muscles which exacerbate this tight breathing. As a performer, you must learn the proper method of deep breathing.

It is also important to know where to breathe. For proper relaxation, one should inhale through the nose, because the nose acts as a natural air filter, and exhale out your mouth, giving you a more forceful release. As you inhale, I want you to think about a count of 4-6; and then as you exhale, think about a count of 6-8, making your exhalation a little bit longer than your inhalation.

SCRIPT FOR THE 5-4-3-2-1 RELAXATION SESSION

This is a script that you can read to your team to help them practice and develop the skill of relaxation. You will want to read it slowly and in a monotone voice.

The first thing you want to do is put yourself in a quiet, comfortable environment. Sit up straight in your chair, hands in your lap or on the desk in front of you, feet flat on the floor. Please look at a spot on the wall in front of you, and focus on that spot.

Now, let your eyes gently close as you inhale, breathing deeply through your nose. As you inhale, your shoulders and chest should not move. Focus on breathing steadily and deeply through the nose, pushing out all your abdominal muscles as your diaphragm expands and air fills the bottom of your lungs. Now, exhale through your mouth, as your abdominal muscles and diaphragm contract and the air exits your lungs.

As you continue to focus on your breathing, having a count of 4-6 on the inhalation and 6-8 on the exhalation, realize that everything you need to relax is already inside you. The world's most powerful tranquilizers lay within. The ability to relax is a skill that needs to be developed and you are doing that now. You need to train to relax just like you do for the skills required to play hockey.

Answer the following three questions as you continue to focus on your breathing. Answer these questions in your mind and notice how the answers just pop into your head:

1. What is 3 x 3?

2. What is your middle name?

3. What street did you grow up on?

Notice how easily and effortlessly the answers popped into your mind. The ability to relax is a skill that can be trained, developed and called upon just as easily as answering those three questions.

We will now go through a short body scan in which you are to focus your awareness into the body parts that are mentioned.

When you hear the number 5, let your toes, the balls of your feet, arches, heels, your ankles, your Achilles tendon, your calves and your shins release, relax and let go.

When you hear the number 4, let your knees, your quads, your hamstrings, your gluteus maximus, your groin, your hips, your whole lower body release, relax and let go, sinking further and further into the chair that you are sitting on.

When you hear the number 3, let your lower back, your mid back, your upper back, your abs, your obliques, your ribs, your pectorals, your whole torso release, relax and let go.

What you will find is that the more relaxed you become, the better you might feel; and the better you feel, the more relaxed you will want to become.

When you hear the number 2, relax your traps, your shoulders, your biceps, your triceps, your forearms, your hands, your fingers – just release, relax and let go.

When you hear the number 1, relax the back of your neck, the back of your head, the top of your head, your forehead, your eyes, your cheeks, your jaw; let your lips gently part and your tongue hang in your mouth as a complete and total body of relaxation takes over.

What you will realize is that the more relaxed you become, the better you will feel; and the better you feel, the more relaxed you will want to become.

Take another deep breath.

Now, gently open your eyes and bring yourself back to this moment, right here, right now.

This concludes the 5-4-3-2-1 relaxation session.

CONTROL THE ENVIRONMENT

In order to properly condition your relaxation, you must begin training in a controlled environment. Initial relaxation training should occur in a quiet and controlled environment where you can relax in peace. This enables you to focus on the process of relaxation in that moment, ignoring all other stimuli and emptying the mind of unnecessary thoughts.

After you have practiced in this controlled and quiet environment for a few weeks, slowly integrate adversity to simulate a more chaotic or competitive environment similar to a hockey game.

Introduce crowd noise or music in the background of your controlled setting and practice your relaxation response to this adversity by focusing on your breathing. Audio simulates adversities that will become distractions if you let them get into your head. Do not let them get in your head; instead, focus on the next breath. Use your relaxed state of mind to push distractions far away by locking into what you want to focus on, going one breath at a time.

Once you have trained your ability to relax under simulated adversity in a controlled environment, the next step is to perform your relaxation technique in performance practices, and then pressure-packed scenarios in game-like practices. During these preparation sessions, you will further practice the execution of your relaxation techniques, and eventually this will translate to an execution and peak performance during games.

CONTROL YOURSELF

As I am sure you have gathered by now, breathing is the foundation for relaxation. Simultaneously, breathing is the basis for emotional state management, aka self-control. Relaxation conditions self-control by teaching you how to become grounded within the self. Your body and mind become one in the present moment as you focus on the breathing. The relaxation process is proven to reduce stress levels and alleviate anxiety, giving you control of your emotional state. Good breathing makes all the difference in self-control, and thus in the achievement of performance excellence.

CONDITIONING THE RELAXATION RESPONSE

If you have never trained your breathing and you try to relax by taking a deep breath in a pressure situation, the body and the brain will not be conditioned to respond by gaining control of yourself. If you condition yourself to relax through the routine practice of deep breathing, first in the quiet, controlled environment and then in more disruptive scenarios, by the time you call upon it in the heat of competition on the ice, it will be a skill you have developed and it will be there when you need it.

When you practice the 5-4-3-2-1 technique, you will feel more connected to the present moment, more relaxed and more in control of yourself. The more you train with the 5-4-3-2-1 technique, the more you focus on your breathing and the more you do your relaxation training, the more this relaxation preparation is going to help in practices and games. The goal is for this technique to become so routine that when you take a deep breath to help you relax, your body will be conditioned to respond by relaxing and getting you in a place of self-control. When this occurs, you will know you have a properly conditioned relaxation response.

RELAXATION IN THE RECOVERY PROCESS

For hockey players to take their performance to the next level, they must constantly put their bodies and minds in uncomfortable and stressful situations where they are challenged to adapt and evolve. To consistently bring a high level of energy and effort to these situations, players must be able to recover outside of the competitive arena.

Relaxation is a tremendous facilitator of recovery. The more relaxed you are, the greater the recovery process, thus assisting your physical and mental regeneration so that you can continue to compete and train at your highest level.

RECOVERY PROCESS

As you are probably well aware, there is a physical recovery process after physical performance in which the body goes to work repairing the damage done to muscle tissue. After a weight lifting session, it is this physical recovery process that builds the muscle you desire for performance. Not surprisingly, there is a mental recovery process of releasing performance stress and anxiety that is equally important. In the process, these two forms of recovery often converge, blending similar practices and exercises to maximize both forms of recovery. All athletes should be aware of the significance of recovery on performance and understand that both your physical and mental recoveries are enhanced when in a relaxed state.

CAIN'S COACHING POINT:

If you were to grade your ability to relax on a 1-10 scale, with 10 being the best, you would give yourself a grade of ?

1 2 3 4 5 6 7 8 9 10

To help me move one number closer to 10, I will do the following:

_____

_____

THE MAGIC 20-MINUTE WINDOW OF RECOVERY

Dr. Declan Connolly is a world-renowned exercise physiologist, sports nutritionist, and strength and conditioning coach. He is a professor at The University of Vermont and a consultant to the New York Rangers, among other professional teams and Olympic organizations. He also was my college undergraduate advisor at The University of Vermont and remains to this day a close personal friend and mentor on the physiological aspects of performance. Dr. Connolly speaks of the importance of the sports nutrition magic 20-minute window.

The magic 20-minute window of sports nutrition indicates that you want to have food in your system, whether it is a protein shake, a peanut butter and jelly sandwich or even a Snickers bar, within the 20-minute period after finishing a workout to help speed up the recovery process.

The recovery benefits of getting food in your system within 20 minutes after the completion of a workout will be greater than if you had steak and potatoes 45 minutes to 1 hour after a workout. Physically and mentally, the recovery process is kick-started when you can get these much-needed proteins, carbohydrates, and fats into your system within that window. Developing the discipline to bring food with you for post-performance snacks is important to enhance your recovery process. It is equally important that you force yourself to act on your knowledge of recovery, because many athletes report they do not feel like eating after performance. If you let your feelings dictate your actions, you lose in hockey and in life.

DISCIPLINE IS THE KEY TO RECOVERY

The hardest part about eating inside of the magic 20-minute window after completing a workout is having the discipline to bring food with you to the gym or the rink. Establishing a disciplined routine of bringing yourself a simple peanut butter and jelly sandwich on wheat bread, or a piece of fruit, and getting that food in your system within that 20-minute window will dramatically speed up your recovery process.

ONE-THIRD OF YOUR LIFE – INVEST IN A BED

If you knew you were going to spend one-third of your life performing a sport, you would want to gather all the information you could and educate yourself on how to achieve performance excellence in that sport. If you knew you were going to work a specific job for one-third of your life, I bet you would also want to become as knowledgeable and proficient as possible to achieve job performance excellence. So why would sleep, which you will do for approximately one-third of your life, be any different? Unfortunately, you probably know very little about what goes on physiologically when you sleep, so let's get you started with some general knowledge about the importance of sleep for your recovery. It is the #1 most important factor and place that you can get a competitive advantage.

POWER SLEEP

Dr. James Maas is a professor at Cornell University and one of the world's leading authorities and experts on sleep. In his book *Power Sleep*, he breaks down the information you need to know about sleeping and how much you need it to perform at your peak. As a scholar, he has addressed the physiological benefits of sleep and the issue of severe sleep deprivation that plagues most college and high school athletes, resulting in performances that represent about 80% of their potential.

An individual is considered to be sleep deprived if he or she sleeps four hours or less per night, while eight hours constitutes normal sleep. The National Sleep Foundation's sleep guidelines recommend seven to nine hours for the average adult. Dr. Maas suggests in *Power Sleep* that you get 9 hours and 15 minutes of sleep a night so that you will receive your five REM (Rapid Eye Movement) cycles, thus maximizing the physiologic benefits of your recovery time in sleep. One night of missed sleep will probably do little harm, but the cumulative effect of poor sleep will have a negative impact on your performance.

Sleep is an active physiological process, one in which your body is busy carrying out vital activities while you are unconscious. While asleep, your body alternates between two forms of sleep: rapid eye movement (REM) and non-REM sleep. This cycle repeats several times throughout the night. The stage of REM sleep provides the brain with the energy to support it during waking hours and is necessary for restoring the mind to function at a level of peak performance. These physiological processes are significant for your psyche, because mental conditioning is most effective when an individual's psychological state is in sync with an optimum physiological state.

10 TIPS FOR SOUND SLEEPING

1. **RELAX BEFORE RETIRING** – Take some time for a pre-sleep ritual to break the connection between stress and bedtime. Try listening to the 5-4-3-2-1 relaxation session, listen to relaxation music, do some light stretching or take a hot shower.

2. **WATCH THE CAFFEINE** – Caffeine is the stimulant present in coffee (100-200 mg), soda (50-75 mg), tea (50-75 mg), and various over-the-counter medications. Caffeine should not be consumed for at least four to six hours before bedtime.

3. **WATCH THE ALCOHOL** – Although alcohol is a depressant and may help you fall asleep, the subsequent metabolism that clears it from your body when you are sleeping causes a withdrawal syndrome. This withdrawal causes awakenings and is often associated with nightmares and sweats. To help reduce some of these effects, try drinking one glass of water for every alcoholic beverage consumed. You should stop all liquid consumption at least two hours before bedtime so that you are not waking up in the middle of the night to urinate.

4. **EXERCISE AT THE RIGHT TIME** – Regular exercise relieves stress and encourages good sleep. However, if a little exercise really gets your blood pumping, it would be wise to avoid working out in the evening or just before bedtime.

5. **CUT DOWN ON NOISE, LIGHT, EXTREME TEMPERATURES** – Try earplugs, a night-light, an eye mask or drape clip. The best temperature for sleep is 65-69 degrees.

6. **EAT RIGHT AND SLEEP TIGHT** – Avoid eating a large meal just before bedtime or going to bed hungry. It is about balance. Also, whenever possible, opt for foods that promote sleep, such as milk, tuna, halibut, artichokes, oats, asparagus, potatoes and bananas.

7. **UNDERSTANDING JET LAG** – Before you cross time zones, try waking up later or earlier to help your body adjust to the time difference. It takes approximately one day for each hour you fly to adjust to a new time zone. Many people are affected more severely by West to East travel than East to West. Anticipate that it may take a few days for your body to catch up, and you can speed up that process by easing yourself on the new time zone schedule before you leave.

8. **RESPECT THE PURPOSE OF THE BED** – Avoid TV, eating, and emotional discussions while in bed. The mind and body associate bedtime activities with being in bed. Do not let a bad habit keep you awake.

9. **NAP SMART** – A power nap early in the afternoon can really refresh you. Make it brief – no more than 20 minutes. Sleep too much and you may spend the night staring at the ceiling.

10. **PET SLEEPERS** – Does your pet sleep with you? This, too, may cause arousals from either allergies or their movements in the bed – Fido and Kitty may be better off on the floor than on your sheets.

Be sure to invest in the best mattress you can afford. How you spend the eight hours a night you invest in bed will determine how you are able to invest the other 2/3 of your life that day. Invest in yourself. Invest in your rest and recovery. Invest in the best mattress you can buy.

OLYMPIC SLEEP TRICKS

The USA Olympic organization will often go into the Olympic Village ahead of the games and put in extended-length beds and blackout curtains in the rooms of all its athletes. This is because the organization recognizes how important sleep is to its athletes' peak performance. The USOC wants to give our athletes the best opportunity to bring home the gold and so it invests wisely in sleep.

You probably cannot travel with blackout curtains, but you can get a pair of earplugs and an eye mask for under $10.00. If you are a high school or college student and you are living in a dorm where people come home late at night slamming doors, roommates make noise and there is a constant commotion, make the investment in your sleep time by getting earplugs that will block much of that noise and an eye mask to shut out the excess light. Both items will help with your ability to get an excellent night's sleep. You may also want to try one of the many sleep noise apps on your phone.

CAIN'S EXPENSIVE EXPERIENCE ON RECOVERY

When I was an athlete, I always thought I was capable of more than was requested of me and that the longer and harder I worked, the better I would become. I was constantly working out and running, doing more than was expected. What I failed to realize was the significant difference between working harder versus working smarter, and that the more I worked, the more I needed to recover.

I never had a plan for recovery or for a great sleep routine and probably slept around 4-6 hours a night in college. As a result, I broke down physically and mentally, and I was injured all the time. I was the guy who pulled all-nighters, thinking I could cram all my studying into one or two days and then regurgitate it on exam day. I would either take course exams so jacked up on caffeine that I would crash in the middle of them, or I would walk in and simply not recall any of the information because I was so tired. If you are a casualty of poor recovery habits, *Power Sleep* can help you with its review of the physiological and psychological problems that come with pulling all-nighters.

YOGA AS A MENTAL CONDITIONING EXERCISE

Again, it was my course with Coach Bruening that turned my life and recovery routines in a productive and progressive direction. In this course, Coach Bruening taught yoga to the class as a source of both physiological and psychological relaxation. Practicing and understanding the benefits of yoga have really helped me become more familiar with my body and in managing my emotional state. During that course, I improved my flexibility and learned how to breathe and find my center of balance, both physically and mentally.

Ironically, before the 2013-2014 NFL season there was a fantastic article on ESPN.com about the Seattle Seahawks and how they used yoga as a part of their pre-practice routine to gain better control of their breath and their physical/mental/emotional self.

RE-CENTER YOURSELF

Relaxation and recovery are both critical elements within a peak performer's mental conditioning program. Training your relaxation response through deep breathing will help you stay locked into the present moment, think more clearly, and perform more fluidly during competition. Relaxation outside of the competitive arena will help you speed up the recovery process, enabling you to return and perform harder, longer and smarter as you take your hockey performance to the next level.

Throughout life, it is important to use these relaxation and recovery practices to constantly re-center yourself, because internal balance leads to the performance consistency necessary for all peak performers. As you climb The Mountain of Hockey Excellence, remember to pause, take a deep breath and re-center yourself. This pause will keep you climbing at your most productive pace and playing hockey one shift at a time.

MENTAL IMAGERY

At this moment, imagine standing on a stage that is situated in an enormous arena. As you look around, you suddenly realize the air is being filled by thunderous applause reverberating around the arena. The arena is full of people and they are standing up out of their seats. As you remain on the stage, taking in the sights and the sounds, you realize this standing ovation is for you.

It is a trophy ceremony at the championship parade and you are the MVP! You turn to your right and left and high five and hug your jubilant teammates. You seek out your coach for more celebration and then you look out into the stands for your family. It is a moment like no other!

A voice over the loudspeaker announces the beginning of the trophy presentation. The trophy is handed over to the head coach, who passes it to the assistant coaches, and then it makes its way to the players.

As you get your hands on the trophy, you raise it above your head, the crowd responds with another great wave of applause, and you return the acknowledgement with a smile. As you stand there with the physical manifestation of the title, a final and total comprehension of your achievement washes over you. This is it. In this moment, you have reached the mountaintop.

There on the stage, you stand at the pinnacle of hockey at your level. You stand a champion. With utmost satisfaction, you know you have given your best when you needed it the most and that your performance has been simply superior to the competition. Your PRIDE – that Personal Responsibility In Daily Excellence, your making all of your todays count and not counting them over all those years of training – has culminated in this. The game has rewarded that PRIDE. Now, all the world watches and recognizes you as the ultimate peak performer, the epitome of performance excellence when it comes to hockey.

This imaginary scenario is your introduction to mental imagery. Now, let's make that vision a reality.

CAIN'S COACHING POINT:

Everything happens twice. First in your mind, and then in reality. Mental Imagery is one of the most well-researched mental skills that is NOT being used in hockey on a consistent basis. That means Mental Imagery is a place where you can get a competitive advantage and take your game to the next level.

HEAD REHEARSAL

One of the most underutilized mental conditioning skills in all of hockey is mental imagery. Mental imagery, often referred to as visualization, is the process of creating mental experiences that resemble actual physical experiences. Similar to watching a highlight video of your best performance in your mind.

This process is similar to the stimulation of the imagination when you read an excerpt in the second-person narrative, such as the introduction to this chapter. The difference is that the script is not on a piece of paper in front of you; it is all in your head.

In mental conditioning, mental imagery is used to enhance performance preparation and build confidence. It is a technique employed to exercise the mind by mentally creating the environment of performance competition and mentally performing the competitive tasks required in hockey in your mind. Mentally, you rehearse how you want to feel and how you want to perform, imagining the integration of your physical conditioning and your mental conditioning within your mind to see your best performance before you step out on the ice for battle.

THE MIND-BODY CONNECTION

Mental imagery has the potential to make a HUGE impact in your hockey performance. Whether you vividly imagine or you physically execute your performance, the brain processes those two experiences with similar psychoneuromuscular pathways. Made simple, you hardwire your brain and body for peak performance.

Mental imagery is physiologically creating neural patterns in your brain in the same manner as the performance of a physical action. Essentially, if you are lying in bed at night and you practice mental imagery, you are imprinting the blueprint of your performance in your mind – further embedding those pathways and enhancing your capacity to achieve what it is you see in your mind when you step onto the ice.

CAIN'S COACHING POINT:

Before you get carried away, however, let's get one thing clear: Mental imagery is not a substitute for physical preparation. This is not some shortcut or fast track to peak performance. Putting in the physical time is necessary. The mental conditioning technique of mental imagery enhances your physical abilities by deepening those psychoneuromuscular pathways in your brain. Mental imagery is utilized to maximize the efficiency and effectiveness of your physical preparation.

YOU ARE "THE ARCHITECT" OF YOUR VISION

In order to emphasize how an individual practices mental imagery, I've drawn a parallel to it and a concept from the Warner Brothers blockbuster movie *Inception.* In the film, a complex plot revolves around dreams and characters' movements in and out of the dream world. There are particular characters in the movie called "architects," who build infinitely detailed dream worlds that mirror reality. This movie is one of the ultimate mind-benders in cinema, and if you haven't seen it, I apologize for using this particular analogy. However, this concept of "architects" is exactly what you want to emulate in your process of mental imagery.

When you perform the mental conditioning technique of mental imagery, you create a mental world. You construct in your mind a psychological replica of your sport's competitive arena (locker room, on-ice, etc.), placing you and your opponent within that arena and lining up at center ice. When you perform mental imagery, you want to build in the sense of sight, the sense of sound, and the sense of touch. You want to mentally experience the appearance of where you will be playing, the rink, and the uniforms of your opponent.

You want to experience the energy in the rink. If you are playing away from home, imagine the away crowd heckling you from the stands. You want to experience yourself making the plays that will make the difference at game's end. Some athletes even integrate the familiar smells of their venue or the locker room into their mental imagery. The more details you construct as the architect of the video in your mind, the greater you enhance the effectiveness of the mental imagery experience.

PHYSIOLOGICAL BENEFITS FROM PSYCHOLOGICAL STIMULUS

If you are still a little skeptical about mental imagery, then I want to give you a little taste of the mind-body connection. I want you to experience the physiological response to the psychological stimulus of mental imagery. Before telling you to just go off and practice mental imagery, I will walk you through a scenario.

Whenever you perform mental imagery, recall and practice the techniques of relaxation to help you focus more clearly on the mental imagery process.

So sit back and focus on your breathing. Go through the process of relaxation and practice your deep breathing as you read the passage below, or have someone read it to you.

I am going to walk you through a scenario where you go into your kitchen, reach into your refrigerator, pull out a lemon, cut lemon wedges, and take a bite out of one of those lemon wedges. Read slowly and imagine the scenario in all its detail. Practice utilizing all your senses in this passage, because you want to make this scenario feel as real as possible in your mind.

THE LEMON EXPERIMENT

Start by taking 3 good breaths on a 4-6 count on your inhalation and on a 6-8 count on exhalation. Breathe in nice and deep through your nose and release out through your mouth.

Now, imagine walking into your kitchen at home. Feel what the floor feels like on your bare feet.

You are now standing in front of your refrigerator. See the refrigerator in front of you in all its detail. Now, extend your hand outward, reaching for the refrigerator door, and clasp its door handle.

As you open that refrigerator door, notice a nice big, bright yellow lemon on the top shelf.

Reach for it and grab it. As you hold it in the palm of your hand, see the skin and feel the coolness and texture of that lemon as you feel its weight in your hand.

Put that lemon on the counter, take a knife lying there, and use it to cut the lemon in half the long way. See the juice and the body of that lemon as the knife slices through. Smell the slightly sour scent released into the air. Take half of the cut lemon and cut it again, so that you have two equal wedges. See and feel the sting of the lemon juice on your wet fingertips. Breathe in that lemon scent swelling in the air.

Now gently place your fingers, wet with lemon juice, on either side of a lemon wedge and lift it off the counter. Bring it up to your mouth and close your lips around the wedge before sinking your teeth along the lemon rind and squeezing the lemon juice into your mouth. Feel the lemon juice squirt onto the back of your tongue and the back of your mouth. Feel that sensation at the back of your teeth as you press your tongue against them to get all the lemon juice.

Remove the lemon and place the deflated wedge back on the counter.

A TASTE OF THE IMAGE

Did you have a bit of a puckering sensation? Did your mouth salivate at the thought of the lemon taste? Could you smell that lemon or feel the sour juice sting your taste buds? Just thinking about the process of eating lemon made me salivate while I wrote this passage.

If you did receive any of those sensations as you read the passage, then you have now consciously experienced a physiological response (the body responding) to a psychological stimulus. This is a simple firsthand experience that emphasizes the shared psychoneuromuscular pathways of the brain and body. Remember this experience and try to simulate the realness of eating the lemon in your mental imagery when you visualize yourself playing your best hockey.

If you did not experience a physiological response, then you probably read the passage too fast and didn't immerse yourself in this psychological scenario... or maybe you just did not eat enough lemons as a kid! But seriously, in order to properly utilize mental imagery, you MUST use the techniques of relaxation that you have learned. You must become absolutely immersed in the present mental rehearsal you are performing, releasing all mental bricks and deflecting all distractions.

MENTAL REHABILITATION & MENTAL REPS

One of the best ways to maintain your edge while recovering from an injury is to use mental imagery to take mental reps. If you cannot practice hockey, there is no reason why you cannot mentally prepare yourself for physical performance. Often called mental reps, players use mental imagery to imagine themselves doing all of the physical skills they would be doing that day in practice – a line rush with your line mates, getting a clear picture in your mind of what that entry will look like before it happens, and then checking to see if you had the clear image of the right play. This mental rehabilitation really provides a huge psychological advantage in the physical rehabilitation process by keeping the performance-specific psychoneuromuscular pathways in your brain active and as sharp as possible.

When a player is finally physically ready to perform, those psychoneuromuscular pathways are as close to game-ready as they can possibly be. By maintaining active psychoneuromuscular pathways, there is no dusting off the mental cobwebs and there is no regaining your mental edge. Your brain has been mentally preparing during the whole process of rehab and is fit and ready for performance on the ice. By knowing how to practice mental imagery, there is absolutely no reason to lose your mental edge and confidence of knowing the plays or what your alignment and assignment are for that play.

MENTAL IMAGERY PAYS BIG DIVIDENDS

Michael Jordan once said: "I visualized where I wanted to be, what kind of player I wanted to become. I knew exactly where I wanted to go, and I focused on getting there." To read a perspective such as this from a legend like Michael Jordan is a testament to the importance of mental imagery for success in hockey or any sport. Michael Jordan, who was cut from the varsity team his sophomore year in high school, became the first basketball player worth $1 billion, in 2014. So as you can see, mental imagery pays big dividends.

MENTAL PERFORMANCE
BEFORE PHYSICAL PERFORMANCE

Mental imagery can help increase an athlete's performance because the mind can do the skill without actually physically doing that particular skill. Therefore, a hockey player can improve his or her overall skills through mental imagery. A player who wants to improve in scoring can take a few minutes and mentally "imagine" being a successful goal scorer. Each step in the shooting process can be visualized and experienced through imagery.

VIDEO ENHANCEMENT

I cannot emphasize enough that when you are doing mental imagery, you want to make the experience as game-like as possible. You want to utilize all of your mental capacity to make the images appear vivid and clear. A technique sometimes used to assist mental imagery is watching video of yourself performing before you do mental imagery. Witnessing yourself play on tape is not only good for understanding how you perform, but also can aid the practice of mental imagery since using past performances to conjure images helps provide details to mentally rehearse future performances.

I encourage the athletes I work with to create a personal highlight video that they watch before they do mental imagery. This enables them to relive their best performances and then re-imagine their feelings in those scenarios through mental imagery.

PRACTICING ADVERSITY

A great way to utilize the benefits of mental imagery is to create a list of situations in your sport that make you uncomfortable and represent some form of adversity. Once you have made this list, use it as a checklist and use mental imagery to perform under each adverse scenario, executing exactly the way you want to in performance. This is similar to the favorite physical practice of children acting out a last-second scenario, where their team is down one and they make the game-winning shot as time expires. Both practices deal with adverse situations and both imagine a desired outcome.

IMAGINE YOUR EXCELLENCE

Mental imagery is one of most basic and fundamental of all mental conditioning strategies; however, it is widely underused. Remember that actions speak louder than words. You now have a greater understanding of the power of mental imagery; you just need to DO mental imagery in order to increase your performance preparation and confidence.

4 STEPS OF MENTAL IMAGERY

Doing mental imagery is as easy as you closing your eyes and watching your human highlight reel in your mind. It does not need to get more complex than that. When I train coaches to take their teams through mental imagery the night before games, I outline four steps so that they have a rhythm and routine to follow.

1. **RELAXATION** – Take them through the 5-4-3-2-1 technique.

2. **CONFIDENCE CONDITIONING** – Take players through the positive affirmations you want them to hear and that you want to embed into their mental game. Say each statement three times with enough time between statements so that the players can repeat them to themselves.

3. **MENTAL RECALL** – Have the players recall and revisit their best hockey performances of all time. They replay those big hits and great plays in their minds as if the past were happening now.

4. **MENTAL REHEARSAL** – Have the players go forward to their next performance and visualize how exactly they want to perform. You can talk them through very specific situations that you have been preparing for against your upcoming opponent.

MENTAL IMAGERY WHILE WATCHING FILM

Another great time to use mental imagery is while you are watching film. A great film-watching routine is to:

1. Show the name of the system or tactic you are about to show. If defense, show how the opponent attacks and what they are doing.

2. Players imagine executing exactly like they want to on that play.

3. Roll the play so you can see what actually happened.

4. Players grade themselves on their performance before any coach says anything so that the players have to take ownership and are more engaged in the film breakdown process.

5. Have players imagine executing the play exactly the way they should have so that they get the "corrective mental rep."

6. Then break down the play in as much detail as you can by asking questions of the players so they have to go inside of their own heads and search for the answer, making them more engaged in the learning process.

Following these six steps for each play should take around 1 minute per play if the coach has prepared the right way. Incorporating mental imagery into teaching through video is a great way to speed up the learning curve, and it dramatically enhances the effectiveness of your video sessions.

CHAPTER #9 REVIEW

- We all possess the ability to relax.

- Aim to perform with a relaxed intensity.

- Relaxation is the secret to results under pressure.

- Relaxation is a skill one must develop like any other physical skill.

- Diaphragmatic breathing is superior to shoulder breathing.

- Practice the 5-4-3-2-1 technique to build a relaxation response.

- Begin training your relaxation response in a controlled environment and progress under simulated adversity.

- Emotional state management is all about self-control and breathing.

- Relaxation is instrumental to recovery process.

- Invest in your sleep.

- Relaxation before bed facilitates productive sleep, benefiting physiological and psychological recovery.

- Mental conditioning is most effective when an individual's psychological state is reflective of an optimum physiological state.

- Internal balance leads to the performance consistency necessary for all peak performers.

- You cannot make yourself relax; you must *let* yourself relax.

- Mental imagery is the process of creating mental experiences that resemble physical experience.

☐ Mental performance physiologically creates neural patterns in your brain in the same manner as the performance of physical action.

☐ As a mental architect, you want to build experiences of all the senses within your mental performance.

☐ Mental imagery enhances psychoneuromuscular pathways to assist physical rehabilitation.

☐ Practice mental performance before beginning physical competition.

☐ Watching videos of your best performances benefits your mental imagery by giving you a positive visual.

☐ Practice handling adversity in mental imagery as you do during preparation.

CHAPTER #10

INSPIRATION & MOTIVATION

"The 'final score' is not the final score. My final score is how prepared you were to execute near your own particular level of competence, both individually and as a team. The bottom line is did we compete at our highest level? That is the controllable. The outcome is not."

Jason Kersner
Head Hockey Coach
Skipjacks Hockey

I was in Dallas, Texas, at a fair and on a stage was a big, muscular strongman performing some amazing feats of strength. He was ripping phone books in half and bending crowbars with his hands to the thunderous applause of his audience.

In one of his acts, he pulled out a lemon and squeezed all the juice out of that lemon and said: "Ladies and gentlemen, I am a strongman. I've squeezed all the juice out of this lemon. I will give $1,000 to anyone who can come up and extract one more drop."

In response, two giant Dallas Cowboy-like guys went on stage to give it a try. The first guy grabbed the lemon and gave it a good, hard squeeze. No drop!

The crowd laughed in amusement as he stepped back to let his friend give the lemon a squeeze. The crowd went silent and watched the second guy give the lemon a squeeze, contorting his face in grimaced concentration. He suddenly released his grip with a gasp for air, but still not one drop of lemon juice.

The crowd laughed and applauded as the two men exited the stage. The strongman was left on stage holding his arms in the air with the lemon in his hand when he saw an old lady, who looked to be in her seventies, walking up the stairs onto the stage.

The strongman said: "Ma'am, for the sake of time, can we move on? You are not going to squeeze any juice out of the lemon. I mean, c'mon. The guys who just tried couldn't do it and they looked like professional football players."

"Sir, just give me a chance," the old lady said politely.

"Okay. Here you go. One chance," said the strongman, who handed her the lemon as the crowd cheered in support.

The old lady took the lemon within her hands and began to squeeze. Her face became contorted. Her jaw set. Her veins began popping out of her forehead. Her glasses fell off her face. Her entire body shook back and forth from her intense struggle with the lemon as she squeezed it with all her might.

BOOM!!

Out popped one drop of lemon juice!!!

The audience erupted in applause! The sounds of clapping, whistles and cheers rang throughout the fair. The strongman was blown away as he was compelled to show the audience the plate on which the drop of lemon juice had fallen. The old lady stood there onstage with her hands on her knees as she collected her breath. It was a scene to behold.

Then the strongman walked over with a check he had just written out for $1,000 and handed it to the lady as he said: "Ma'am, you have got to tell us. I've never had anyone squeeze an extra drop of juice out of that lemon. How did you do it?"

She replied: "Sir, I have to tell you. I am 74 years old. I just lost my husband. I've got three grandchildren that we're raising and I just lost my job. I needed that money."

The old lady was inspired. She was motivated. She had a reason WHY she needed to squeeze that juice out of the lemon. **With a big enough reason why, you will always find a way how.**

Your reason why is the fuel that burns the fire of inspiration and motivation inside of you.

So what is your "why"? Why do you do what you do? Why are you reading this right now? What do you want to accomplish in your life, this season, this week, today? What is your process for making those dreams a reality?

Most people think inspiration and motivation are things that you can do once in a while by reading a book, watching a movie or hearing a motivational speaker. Most people think that is all it takes for you to stay motivated. Realistically, that could not be farther from the truth. Although those experiences may spark a flame, in order to fan the flame and make it burn with a passion, you must have a BIG reason why.

> "Nothing great was ever achieved without ENTHUSIASM."
>
> ### *Ralph Waldo Emerson*

MOTIVATION IS A DAILY DECISION

Imagine only brushing your teeth once a week. I hope, for everyone's sake, that you are disgusted by the thought of brushing your teeth only once a week! Your teeth would become yellow, feel hairy and would develop cavities and/or rot. In addition, nobody would want to hold a conversation with you because your breath would blow them away. My point is that you cannot brush your teeth once a week or take a bath once a week and expect your teeth to look good and you to smell good.

Inspiration and motivation work the same way as dental hygiene, except they are not for your oral health but for your mental performance health. You should mentally absorb some form of inspiration daily to motivate you in your preparation and performance. Do not read something inspiring once a week. Do not motivate yourself or your team once or even a couple times a week. Inspiration and motivation must be performed every single day.

THE DAILY DOMINATOR & HOCKEY

This is why I wrote the book *The Daily Dominator*. With The DOMINATOR you get to read one page a day of mental conditioning material so that you can do a little a lot, not a lot a little, and maximize your hockey mental game. Having everyone in your program read the same page each day and then breaking it down at practice or in your positional meetings takes the guesswork out of having to create your own mental conditioning program. Your "do a little a lot" each day is already done; you just have to break it down with your team.

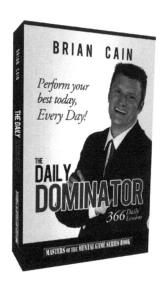

ADVERTISE TO YOURSELF

Have you ever wondered why companies are willing to pay three million dollars for a thirty-second commercial during the Super Bowl? The common response to this question is that tens of millions of people watch the Super Bowl. This is true, but the real reason that advertising works is that advertisements create lasting images within the mind, so that when people go out to consume products, those products from the advertisements jump to the front of their minds.

The same tactics of advertising apply to inspiring peak performance. Advertising to yourself will enhance your preparation and competition by inspiring your performance. Similar to any marketing consultant, before creating sporadic marketing pitches you must know what message or product you are trying to advertise and the most effective methods for marketing that product.

With mental conditioning, the product is the mindset of a peak performer and how that mindset leads to your hockey success. Advertising to yourself through various strategies will help you to create the peak performance mentality you desire and help you to win more games on the ice.

KEVIN YOUNG – OLYMPIC ADVERTISING

The current world record holder in the 400-meter hurdles, with a time of 46.78 seconds, is the 1992 Summer Olympics gold medalist Kevin Young. When Young got to the Olympic Village in Barcelona, he advertised his Olympic goal to himself by writing it down, everywhere. When asked about his preparation in an interview after his world record performance, Young responded by saying: "My goal this year was to run 46.89. I wrote that everywhere in my room, even here up at the Village. I took a pencil and wrote it all on the wall. I integrated it into a lot of things I do at home. I just got into the habit of writing the number around, everywhere I go."

Young used the power of self-advertising his goals by putting his goal in writing, where he could see it often for motivation. As an aspiring peak performer, you too should advertise your goals to yourself by putting them everywhere you can see them. If you truly desire something, you should be able to visualize it as you go through your day at every turn. Self-advertising helps you to focus on what you want, not what you are trying to avoid.

CAIN'S COACHING POINT:

What goals can you write out and post around your room?

_____

_____

SIGNS OF SUCCESS

An excellent habit to develop is collecting inspirational phrases, pictures and images to create "signs of success" to hang around your living space. This provides you with visuals for motivation that you will see on a daily basis. When you see these signs of success every day, it becomes a part of your everyday thought process. After a few days or a week seeing a particular sign, your goal will be to commit this sign of success to memory and, more importantly, to have it effectively motivate you to action.

Players most often self-advertise signs of success by hanging photos, quotes and other images all around their bedroom and locker. Pictures of athletes or coaches who inspire them, quotes that motivate them to continuously check in on their perspective, and mental conditioning statements such as **"Don't count the days, make the days count"** are reminders of the importance of today. Whenever you need them, these inspirational advertisements catch your eye and keep you inspired and motivated on your journey up The Mountain of Hockey Excellence.

The signs of success are simple ways to advertise the peak performance mentality and mental conditioning principles you want to adopt in sport and life.

MAKE YOUR OWN SIGNS OF SUCCESS

Draw from the material and information you have acquired from this book and make your own signs of success. By creating your signs of success, you put your knowledge of peak performance to use and enhance the process of mentally conditioning the habit of excellence.

CAIN'S COACHING POINT:

Based on the content within this manual, what are three captions for signs of success that you will hang in your room to stay inspired?

_____

_____

_____

EXAMPLES OF SELF-ADVERTISEMENT

Now that you know the importance of the signs of success and have created mental game marketing campaigns for yourself, let me share with you what other players have reported hanging in their rooms as signs of success. Remember, at all levels of competition, you are never too young, too old, too bad or too good to stay inspired.

1. A vision board collage of all your goals and what you want to accomplish.

2. A picture of your national or state championship arena where that event will be held.

3. A poster of Muhammad Ali or other athletes who inspire the mentality that you want to develop.

4. A poster of The Miracle on Ice or other great moments in sport that motivate you to do the work it takes so that you too may experience a similar great moment.

5. An inspirational quote from your favorite piece of literature.

BATHROOM MIRROR – DRY ERASE MARKER

Another great technique worth revisiting so you can stay inspired is to write your goals on your bathroom mirror with a dry erase marker. Whenever you enter the bathroom, you will see your goals and be reminded of the mindset you want to develop to become a peak performer. Essentially, your mirror becomes a goal-oriented sign of success.

I have worked with professional mixed martial arts fighters who, immediately upon arriving in Vegas at their hotel room, take out a dry erase marker and write their mental game reminders on the mirror. Writing on their mirror sets the tone for their peak performance mentality; whenever they enter the bathroom, they are reminded of their desired mindset and the need to focus on that mindset and process for performance excellence.

GOAL CARDS CARRIED ALL THE TIME

Another strategy you can use is to carry a card in your wallet with your personal goals displayed on it. Carrying a goal card will make you 35% more likely to make those goals come true because you have constant reinforcement whenever you open your wallet. Whenever you do open your wallet, take a look at that card and mentally check in with how you are moving forward to achieve your goals. This form of self-advertising will go wherever you go.

STICK TAPE ADVERTISING

During preparation or in competition, a great method of self-advertising is to write inspirational messages on the tape on your stick (on the knob where it can be easily read while sitting on the bench). Stick tape is an effective place for self-advertising because you constantly see the messages in front of yourself.

VISION BOARDS

One of the best motivational exercises you can do as an individual and as a team to help with inspiration and motivation is to create a vision board. A vision board is simply a collage of your goals and what you desire to accomplish. I strongly encourage you to create a vision board for yourself, and if you are on a team, I highly recommend you create one together as a team-building and team-focusing exercise.

You will never outperform your self-image. Making a vision board of images will inspire you to accomplish your goals. Place it where you will see it every day. This will keep your goals in the front of your mind and motivate you to achieve them. I personally started using vision boards in 2007 and annually revisit my own board the first week in July. Below is a picture of my personal vision board.

As you can see on my vision board, I want to speak in every state in the country. The ones that are white are the ones where I have not had a chance to speak YET. I want to help teams win national championships (accomplished in 2012). I want to spend more time fishing and hiking in the mountains of Vermont. I want to read at least one book every month. I want to be a better listener. I want to keep my weight under 200 pounds (198lbs at present). I want to have better balance in my life between work and relaxation, and I want to live the core values of being positive, disciplined, progressive and committed to others. I also wanted to be a #1 Best-selling Author (which has been accomplished with my first book *Toilets, Bricks, Fish Hooks and PRIDE*).

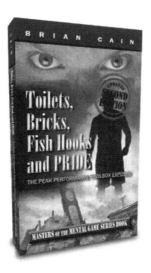

I keep my vision board with me in my binder and I look at it multiple times each week. I have a copy of my vision board on my desk at home and on my desk at the office. The vision board serves as a reminder for me to constantly ask myself: *Is what I am working on right now helping me get to where I want to go?* The vision board is great for helping create the awareness you need to constantly check in on your progress towards achieving your goals and to refocus you on what you want to accomplish.

WORK TO MAKE "IT" WORK

Here's the significant difference between peak performers and the rest of humanity: Peak performers understand that you must work to make "it" work. Whatever that "it" is, it's all about investing time and energy into a process of development that will make you excellent at what you do, and thus will bring you success. The vision board process has worked for me, it has worked for Jack Canfield (author of *Chicken Soup for the Soul*), and it has worked for thousands of other people.

WATCH OUT FOR THE NEGAHOLICS

If you are an unenthusiastic, pessimistic cynic, often referred to as a "Debbie Downer" or a negaholic, and you believe that *"This mental conditioning stuff is bogus, I just want to play"* or *"This stuff is never actually going to improve my performance,"* well, you are right!

Whether you think you can or think you can't, you are right!

Since you have made it this far in the manual, it is clear you are not one of these people. My hope is that, based on all the previous lessons learned in mental conditioning, you can see it is quite apparent this imaginary skeptic obviously has zero knowledge about how peak performance and mental conditioning apply to the journey of excellence in the game of hockey.

What real-life skeptics do not understand is that *you have to work to make it work.* The reason mental conditioning exercises will not work for them is a result of their refusal to try and make it work. It is not rocket science – if you do not attempt to make something work, of course it will not! It is the same logic as the old saying, "You miss 100 percent of the shots you do not take." You must believe in the benefits of mental conditioning for your performance to improve, and there are real, tangible payoffs.

The use of signs of success and vision boards will help you stay focused on your goals, and they will help you to get motivated and stay inspired to DO THE WORK that it takes to be successful.

CAIN'S COACHING POINT:

If you noticed anyone on your team who has openly dismissed mental conditioning and stopped reading this book, reflect on how his attitude and actions affect the team. If his mentality is adversely affecting team chemistry, I suggest confronting him or making your coach aware of the situation as an expression of genuine concern for the team's well-being throughout the season. Sometimes these moments can make all the difference in an athlete's career or even the person's life, because someone took the time and cared enough to step up, maybe more than that person cares about himself.

MOTIVATIONAL MOTION PICTURES

Motivational videos, inspirational movies, and highlight reels are another tremendous tool for peak performers. Similar to the video enhancement in mental imagery, there is no debating that watching some form of motivational motion picture or video before a practice or a game will inspire your performance on that day.

Watching a personal motivational video clip every morning as part of your morning routine also provides great reinforcement for the kind of person and player you want to be today. Regardless of how you feel when you wake up, the video clips you watch will get you fired up to DOMINATE that day and do the work necessary to advance further up The Mountain of Hockey Excellence.

CAIN'S COACHING POINT:

I challenge you to make your own personal highlight video. You can use footage of yourself or of others on YouTube to inspire your performance. Then watch this video on a routine basis.

INSPIRE YOUR DAILY DOMINATION

Whether you read a chapter in this book, watch an inspirational movie clip or use any number of the various methods for inspirational motivation, you must build motivation into your daily routine to become inspired to take action. You will have more success spending 3-5 minutes a day getting inspired and motivated than you will if you spend one hour once a week. Remember, if you get inspired a little a lot, you will have more success than if you get inspired a lot a little.

By the end of using this book, you will possess the information necessary to transform yourself into a peak performing hockey player. It is thus imperative that you motivate yourself to master the mental game in your daily preparation and performance ACTION, not just understand what you should do. Be the one who DOES IT!

Remember, intelligence is acting on the knowledge you have acquired. Use the strategies for motivation and inspiration from within this chapter to inspire your climb up to the summit of The Mountain of Hockey Excellence.

CHAPTER #10 REVIEW

☐ Have a big reason "why" and you will always find a way how.

☐ Make yourself inspired daily by reviewing motivational material.

☐ Advertise your goals to yourself.

☐ Make signs of success for motivation.

☐ Write daily goals on your mirror and make longer-term goal cards.

☐ Self-advertise during performance by writing on stick tape.

☐ Create vision boards for performance goals.

☐ Work to make your goals a reality.

☐ Watch motivational video clips for inspiration.

☐ If you get inspired a little a lot, you will have more success than if you get inspired a lot a little.

CONCLUSION

PERFORMANCE EXCELLENCE

> "Your reputation will not win games. You must be ready mentally and physically one shift at a time every time you step on the ice."
>
> *Jason Kersner*
> *Head Hockey Coach*
> *Skipjacks Hockey*

Excellence is being at your best when it means the most – every single day and every single shift.

This concept rules supreme in peak performance, transcending and penetrating all other aspects of mental conditioning. It is assuming personal responsibility in your daily pursuit of excellence that will make you a champion, because consistency of effort wins. Excellence is about the cultivation of superior mental strength through the process of establishing the proper routines, positive self-talk and a champion's mentality in preparation for inevitable battles through adversity in the game and in life.

After all the mental conditioning material we have covered in this book, you should be both informed and well on your way to achieving your goal of performance excellence in hockey. We have outlined the fundamental principles of mental conditioning and discussed how to adapt these principles and apply them on your journey to the summit of The Mountain of Hockey Excellence. This conclusion explains the purpose of necessary devotion to excellence within performance.

EXCELLENCE IS A LIFESTYLE, NOT AN EVENT

Truly excellent individuals recognize that excellence is not something you do once in a while; you must strive to be excellent all the time – that is, twenty-four hours a day, seven days a week, and three hundred sixty-five days a year. Excellence is a stain you can't wipe off. I hope this book has stained you with excellence.

THREE DOORS & THE LAW OF AVERAGES

You have three doors you can choose to open. You can open the door called WIN, you can open the door called LOSE, or you can open the door called EXCELLENCE. The pursuit of excellence is about more than winning; performance excellence transcends winning. Excellence is a lifestyle; winning is an event that takes place at a moment in time.

Remember that the law of averages says that if you play your best, you give yourself the best chance to win, but you are not guaranteed to win. As a peak performer, you cannot control the outcome; all you can do is work the process to the best of your ability and give yourself the best opportunity for performance success on that day and on that shift. The daily pursuit of excellence is the only way to get there.

THE EXCELLENCE OF BLUE ANGELS

Excellence is about preparing more than other people are willing to and working smarter than other people think is necessary. It is paying close attention to detail within the process in order to give you the results you desire. The Blue Angels are a group of United States Navy Fighter Pilots that perform aerial shows all over the country. What their audiences witness is excellence in motion. What the audience does not see is that the entire performance process demands precision and a commitment to excellence before, and after, they take to the skies.

As some of the most dedicated and excellent performers on the planet, the Blue Angels use mental imagery, video analysis, and a routine brief and debriefing process. Each of these takes about twice as long as the flight itself to prepare for and then learn from each event they perform. The Blue Angels are known for their tight diamond formation in the air, where only 36 inches (just one yard!) separate a plane from its wingtip to the canopy of the other planes (36 inches is about how far your head is from your feet when you sit down and read this). They perform aerial maneuvers at a speed of one mile every 9 seconds or a closure rate, two planes flying directly towards each other at one mile every 4½ seconds – almost 1,000 miles per hour. There is no room for error, and team excellence in their performance is critical.

PURSUIT OF EXCELLENCE OVER PERFECTION

The Blue Angels understand that their pursuit of excellence is different than the pursuit of perfection. They know that there has never been the perfect flight. They are constantly evaluating performance on video, looking for areas of improvement, paying close attention to the details of their flights, and even evaluating the way they march to their airplanes. The Blue Angels team is a model of excellence, and these pilots are truly dedicated to progress and making the team better in their pursuit of excellence TODAY!

When you see the Blue Angels or other peak performers like Wayne Gretzky, Nicklas Lidstrom or Sydney Crosby, they make what they do look very easy and we think they are gifted. Do not be fooled by their grace and proficient performance. Although they may have been blessed with a few faster twitch muscle fibers than Joe Normal, even they have climbed The Mountain of Hockey Excellence one step at a time, and they would be the first to tell you so.

A WORLD CHAMPION STATE OF MIND

Whether you have the physical talent of a world champion or not is irrelevant. Physical skill makes these champions visibly impressive, but more important is their mental toughness. The story behind their physical prowess is the story of their mental prowess – because it is their incredible work ethic, their capacity to embrace adversity, and their insatiable desire to improve to which they owe their success. One of the most beautiful aspects of the mental game is that, regardless of physical skill, you can become a master of the mental game.

Most people believe that you must be great before you can practice like the great ones. Well, most people have got it all wrong. Anyone can execute this program to cultivate the mindset of a champion. You may not lift the same amount of weight or run the same distance, but anyone can prepare and practice with the same mental intensity of a world champion. All physical performance programs should necessarily be tailored to the physical capabilities of the individual, but mental performance programs may be adopted universally. The fundamentals of mental conditioning may be practiced by anyone willing to actively pursue the summit of The Mountain of Hockey Excellence.

THE CLIMB IS THE DISCOVERY

As we have discussed throughout this manual, performance, in sport and in life, is comparable to that of a journey up a mountain. The journey is yours and you alone have the ability to set the tone of your performance to conquer the climb. The mountain you set your sights on is your choice and the journey is your discovery.

Each mountain you approach will require different physical skills that you must master, but the mental skill will remain the same. There will be some mountains that serve as pleasure climbs, while others will challenge your very existence by demanding every ounce of your physical and mental abilities. Sometimes you will be climbing a mountain and you'll realize you no longer wish to reach the summit. Sometimes you will need to return to base camp, take a break and return to conquer the summit at a later date. Each journey up a mountain is a journey of self-discovery, and through each experience you learn a little about yourself and you learn a little bit about the journey. At the end of the day, it is the journey to the summit, not the summit itself, that makes reaching the summit worthwhile.

THE JOURNEY IS THE REWARD,
THE DESTINATION IS THE DISEASE

My hope is that by the end of this book you will have learned how to be an independent, peak performance mountaineer on the ice rink and in life – one who understands that although you may reach the summit of the mountain you are climbing, there is no summit in life and there is no summit to your excellence.

You are on a journey in which the journey is the reward and the destination is the disease. You must understand that every climb is a process and that proper preparation is imperative. You must create a mental road map, detailing where you want to go and who you must become to be worthy of reaching the summit. Remember, if you want more, you must become more.

Becoming more will give you the best chance to reach the summit of any mountain. Once you reach the summit and have thoroughly enjoyed the view, it is time to return to base camp and start climbing another.

CAIN'S COACHING POINT:

There will always be another mountain to climb. Throughout your journeys up the Mountains of Excellence, recognize there is no final summit; there is no finish line. You are on a journey called life and your best bet is to DOMINATE THE DAY, every day, and enjoy this amazing ride.

SUCCESS = THE RESULT OF EXCELLENCE

I have said this before, and I will repeat myself for emphasis. There is no shortcut to performance excellence; there is no easy way to the summit of your mountain. *You don't get the same satisfaction of helicoptering to the summit as you do from climbing.*

Excellence is something you cannot purchase or be gifted, just as success is not something you simply randomly discover. Excellence is the result of a self-transformative journey to becoming more. A journey that you choose to actively endure, and once you develop a strict adherence to personal excellence, you are bound to discover the success you are looking for in *ALL ASPECTS OF YOUR LIFE!*

CAIN'S COACHING POINT:

If you have found value in using this book and if it has helped you in any way, consider giving a copy to five people whom you care about and want to see take their performance to the next level. By giving this book to others, you are helping them find the ideas and mental keys that will unlock their potential. You will help them live a more fulfilled and excellent journey as they climb their Mountain of Excellence. This manual could forever alter the course of someone's life. It could be you who provides the push as a great teammate. Without you, they might never even start hiking.

Write down five people to whom you will give a copy of this manual:

1) _____

2) _____

3) _____

4) _____

5) _____

THE MENTAL CONDITIONS FOR EXCELLENCE

Through this book you have learned many mental conditioning strategies and peak performance principles to help you proceed on your journey to the summit of The Mountain of Hockey Excellence. Regardless of your sport or profession, the utilization of these mental conditioning principles and fundamentals is necessary to help achieve an elite and excellent performance state of mind.

At the conclusion of going through *The Mental Game of Hockey*, you have learned how to:

• Live in the present moment and maximize your time

• Act differently than how you feel and start having good bad days

• Focus on the process over the outcome

• Identify what you can control and what you cannot

• Have your own personal philosophy and core values for life

• Challenge your limiting beliefs and your perspective

• Stay positive in the face of adversity

• Develop preparation and performance routines for a consistently high-level performance

- Take responsibility for your performance and life

- Relax, recover and gain control of your thoughts, feelings and emotions

- Recognize your signal lights and develop the awareness to win

- Release negative thoughts and refocus back to the present when you get distracted

- Move from intelligence and thinking to action and results

- Use mental imagery to help you prepare and be more confident in your performance

- Inspire and motivate yourself to make the impossible possible

- Take action steps to make excellence a lifestyle, not an event

Remember, you will reach the summit of The Mountain of Hockey Excellence by focusing on the next 200 feet. When you take Personal Responsibility In Daily Excellence, everything else will take care of itself. Today, sign your name with excellence on everything and everyone you touch, and I will see you at the summit!

YOUR SIGNATURE HERE   DATE

In Excellence,

Your Mental Conditioning Coach

Brian M. Cain

@BrianCainPeak
www.BrianCain.com

CONCLUSION REVIEW

☐ Excellence is being at your best when it means the most – every single day.

☐ Excellence is a lifestyle, not an event.

☐ You have three doors you can choose to open. You can open the door called WIN, you can open the door called LOSE, or you can open the door called EXCELLENCE.

☐ Excellence is about preparing more than other people are willing to, and working smarter than other people think is necessary.

☐ The pursuit of excellence is constructive; the pursuit of perfection will destroy you.

☐ Anyone can develop a world champion state of mind.

☐ The journey makes reaching the summit worthwhile.

☐ The journey is the reward and the destination is the disease.

☐ Success is the result of excellence.

☐ When you take PRIDE (Personal Responsibility In Daily Excellence) in your performance, everything else will take care of itself.

DOMINATE THE DAY!

ABOUT THE AUTHOR

WHO IS BRIAN M. CAIN?

Brian M. Cain, MS, CMAA, is a #1 best-selling author, speaker, trainer and expert in the fields of Mental Conditioning and Peak Performance. He has worked with coaches, athletes and teams at the Olympic level and in the National Football League (NFL), National Basketball Association (NBA), National Hockey League (NHL), Ultimate Fighting Championship (UFC), and Major League Baseball (MLB).

Cain has also worked with programs in some of the top college athletic departments around the country including the University of Alabama, Auburn University, Florida State University, the University of Iowa, the University of Maryland, the University of Mississippi, Mississippi State University, Oregon State University, the University of Southern California, the University of Tennessee, Vanderbilt University, Washington State University, Yale University, Texas A&M, TCU, Baylor, the University of Georgia, the University of Vermont, and many others.

Cain has worked as a mental conditioning consultant with numerous high school, state and national championship programs. He has delivered his award-winning seminars and presentations at coaches' clinics, leadership summits and athletic directors' conventions all over the country. As a high school athletic director, he is one of the youngest ever to receive the Certified Master Athletic Administration Certification from the National Interscholastic Athletic Administrators Association.

A highly sought-after Peak Performance Coach, clinician, and keynote and motivational speaker, Cain delivers his message with passion and enthusiasm, in an engaging style that keeps his audiences energized while being educated. As someone who lives what he teaches, Cain will inspire you and give you the tools necessary to get the most out of your career.

Please visit www.briancain.com/monday to sign up for his weekly newsletter. Also, visit www.briancain.com/calendar to see when Cain will be in your area so you can experience the benefits of having him come in and work with your team.

WHERE'S CAIN?

Cain's Calendar:

"I want to book Cain when he's in town."

www.BrianCain.com/Monday

www.BrianCain.com/Calendar

ABOUT THE CO-AUTHOR

WHO IS JASON A. KERSNER?

Jason A. Kersner has been coaching top-level Midget teams in the Washington DC/Baltimore region for most of the past decade. Under his leadership his teams became recognized as one of the best Midget programs in the country, as measured in both wins and championships.

During the 2011-2012 season Jason served as head coach of the New Mexico Mustangs of the North American Hockey League (NAHL). After the team went dormant, Jason returned to coaching Midget hockey.

Jason has also been a long-time scout in the USHL. He has worked for the Sioux City Musketeers (2009-2013) and is currently a scout for the Madison Capitols.

In addition to being the founder of the Skipjacks Hockey Club, Jason has been their general manager and head coach for the past three seasons. The Skipjacks Hockey Club fields U16 and U18 teams that compete in the USPHL.

Jason is also co-owner of Pinnacle Performance, an elite training program that creates holistic athletes through a professional approach to player development. The program attracts top hockey players from all over the United States at the Pro, College, Junior and Midget levels.

Jason is a level 5 USA Hockey certified coach, is 32 years of age, and resides in Rockville, MD. He is recognized for his tireless work ethic and his ability to move his players to NCAA Division I programs and the top Junior leagues. He is a master of the mental game while developing a championship culture of winners and learners on the ice and in life.

ADDITIONAL RESOURCES

HOW YOU CAN CONTINUE TO BECOME A MASTER OF THE MENTAL GAME

Available at www.BrianCain.com

Champions Tell All:
Inexpensive Experience From The World's Best
Cain provides you with all access to some of the World's greatest performers. Learn from mixed martial arts world champions and college All-Americans about mental toughness.

The Daily Dominator:
Perform Your Best Today. Every Day!
You get 366 Daily Mental Conditioning lessons to help you start your day down the path to excellence. Investing time each day with Cain is your best way to become your best self.

Toilets, Bricks, Fish Hooks and PRIDE:
The Peak Performance Toolbox EXPOSED
Go inside the most successful programs in the country that use Cain's Peak Performance System. Use this book to unlock your potential and learn to play your best when it means the most.

The Peak Performance System (P.R.I.D.E.)
Personal Responsibility In Daily Excellence
This big, video-based training program is Cain's signature training program for coaches, athletes and teams. It will take you step by step to the top of the performance mountain.

CONNECT WITH CAIN

YOUR LINK TO DOING A LITTLE A LOT, NOT A LOT A LITTLE

 www.twitter.com/briancainpeak

 www.facebook.com/briancainpeak

 www.linkedin.com/briancainpeak

 www.youtube.com/wwwbriancaincom

 www.briancain.com/itunes

SIGN UP FOR BRIAN CAIN'S
MONDAY MENTAL CONDITIONING MESSAGE

Cain's Monday Message is full of information to help you unlock your potential and perform at your best when it means the most. Subscribe for FREE and get a bonus audio training disk: www.BrianCain.com/Monday

CONCENTRATION GRIDS
ONE NUMBER/SHIFT AT A TIME

Brian Cain Peak Performance, LLC
Concentration Training Grid
www.BrianCain.com

86	54	04	72	20	05	34	79	52	17
73	43	50	70	44	12	28	59	94	35
45	62	63	97	51	95	91	67	84	75
27	69	23	00	08	83	09	41	65	78
80	39	68	47	29	93	36	30	38	42
61	53	19	48	49	74	40	18	15	21
60	01	14	22	64	07	58	02	32	16
13	31	26	71	66	33	06	85	10	89
76	46	98	37	99	24	57	11	55	82
92	25	81	96	87	88	77	03	56	90

Brian Cain Peak Performance, LLC
Concentration Training Grid
www.BrianCain.com

86	54	04	72	20	05	34	79	52	17
73	43	50	70	44	12	28	59	94	35
45	62	63	97	51	95	91	67	84	75
27	69	23	00	08	83	09	41	65	78
80	39	68	47	29	93	36	30	38	42
61	53	19	48	49	74	40	18	15	21
60	01	14	22	64	07	58	02	32	16
13	31	26	71	66	33	06	85	10	89
76	46	98	37	99	24	57	11	55	82
92	25	81	96	87	88	77	03	56	90

Brian Cain Peak Performance, LLC
Concentration Training Grid
www.BrianCain.com

86	54	04	72	20	05	34	79	52	17
73	43	50	70	44	12	28	59	94	35
45	62	63	97	51	95	91	67	84	75
27	69	23	00	08	83	09	41	65	78
80	39	68	47	29	93	36	30	38	42
61	53	19	48	49	74	40	18	15	21
60	01	14	22	64	07	58	02	32	16
13	31	26	71	66	33	06	85	10	89
76	46	98	37	99	24	57	11	55	82
92	25	81	96	87	88	77	03	56	90

Brian Cain Peak Performance, LLC
Concentration Training Grid
www.BrianCain.com

86	54	04	72	20	05	34	79	52	17
73	43	50	70	44	12	28	59	94	35
45	62	63	97	51	95	91	67	84	75
27	69	23	00	08	83	09	41	65	78
80	39	68	47	29	93	36	30	38	42
61	53	19	48	49	74	40	18	15	21
60	01	14	22	64	07	58	02	32	16
13	31	26	71	66	33	06	85	10	89
76	46	98	37	99	24	57	11	55	82
92	25	81	96	87	88	77	03	56	90

Brian Cain Peak Performance, LLC
Concentration Training Grid
www.BrianCain.com

86	54	04	72	20	05	34	79	52	17
73	43	50	70	44	12	28	59	94	35
45	62	63	97	51	95	91	67	84	75
27	69	23	00	08	83	09	41	65	78
80	39	68	47	29	93	36	30	38	42
61	53	19	48	49	74	40	18	15	21
60	01	14	22	64	07	58	02	32	16
13	31	26	71	66	33	06	85	10	89
76	46	98	37	99	24	57	11	55	82
92	25	81	96	87	88	77	03	56	90

Brian Cain Peak Performance, LLC
Concentration Training Grid
www.BrianCain.com

86	54	04	72	20	05	34	79	52	17
73	43	50	70	44	12	28	59	94	35
45	62	63	97	51	95	91	67	84	75
27	69	23	00	08	83	09	41	65	78
80	39	68	47	29	93	36	30	38	42
61	53	19	48	49	74	40	18	15	21
60	01	14	22	64	07	58	02	32	16
13	31	26	71	66	33	06	85	10	89
76	46	98	37	99	24	57	11	55	82
92	25	81	96	87	88	77	03	56	90

Brian Cain Peak Performance, LLC
Concentration Training Grid
www.BrianCain.com

86	54	04	72	20	05	34	79	52	17
73	43	50	70	44	12	28	59	94	35
45	62	63	97	51	95	91	67	84	75
27	69	23	00	08	83	09	41	65	78
80	39	68	47	29	93	36	30	38	42
61	53	19	48	49	74	40	18	15	21
60	01	14	22	64	07	58	02	32	16
13	31	26	71	66	33	06	85	10	89
76	46	98	37	99	24	57	11	55	82
92	25	81	96	87	88	77	03	56	90

Brian Cain Peak Performance, LLC
Concentration Training Grid
www.BrianCain.com

86	54	04	72	20	05	34	79	52	17
73	43	50	70	44	12	28	59	94	35
45	62	63	97	51	95	91	67	84	75
27	69	23	00	08	83	09	41	65	78
80	39	68	47	29	93	36	30	38	42
61	53	19	48	49	74	40	18	15	21
60	01	14	22	64	07	58	02	32	16
13	31	26	71	66	33	06	85	10	89
76	46	98	37	99	24	57	11	55	82
92	25	81	96	87	88	77	03	56	90

Brian Cain Peak Performance, LLC
Concentration Training Grid
www.BrianCain.com

86	54	04	72	20	05	34	79	52	17
73	43	50	70	44	12	28	59	94	35
45	62	63	97	51	95	91	67	84	75
27	69	23	00	08	83	09	41	65	78
80	39	68	47	29	93	36	30	38	42
61	53	19	48	49	74	40	18	15	21
60	01	14	22	64	07	58	02	32	16
13	31	26	71	66	33	06	85	10	89
76	46	98	37	99	24	57	11	55	82
92	25	81	96	87	88	77	03	56	90

Brian Cain Peak Performance, LLC
Concentration Training Grid
www.BrianCain.com

86	54	04	72	20	05	34	79	52	17
73	43	50	70	44	12	28	59	94	35
45	62	63	97	51	95	91	67	84	75
27	69	23	00	08	83	09	41	65	78
80	39	68	47	29	93	36	30	38	42
61	53	19	48	49	74	40	18	15	21
60	01	14	22	64	07	58	02	32	16
13	31	26	71	66	33	06	85	10	89
76	46	98	37	99	24	57	11	55	82
92	25	81	96	87	88	77	03	56	90

NOTES PAGE

KEEPING IT ALL IN ONE PLACE

_____

_____

_____

_____

_____

_____

_____

_____

_____

_____

_____

_____

_____

_____

_____

_____

_____

_____

_____

_____

_____

_____

_____

_____

_____

_____

_____

_____

_____

_____

_____

_____

_____

_____

_____

_____

_____

_____

_____

_____

_____

_____

_____

_____

_____

_____

_____

_____

_____

_____

_____

_____

_____

_____

_____

_____

_____

_____

_____

_____

www.BrianCain.com

_____

_____

_____

_____

_____

_____

_____

_____

_____

_____

_____

_____

_____

_____

_____

_____

_____

_____

_____

_____

_____

_____

_____

_____

_____

_____

_____

_____

_____

_____

_____

_____

_____

_____

_____

_____

_____

_____

_____

_____

_____

_____

_____

_____

_____

_____

_____

_____

_____

_____

_____

_____

_____

_____

_____

_____

_____

_____

_____

_____

_____

_____

_____

_____

www.BrianCainInnerCircle.com

Made in the USA
Middletown, DE
21 October 2015